THE
BRIDE VALLEY

Dorset landscape near Litton Cheney. A wood engraving by Reynolds Stone.

The Bride Valley

The story of the past,
with photographs of the present

by C. J. BAILEY

1982

Published by
The Dorset Natural History and Archaeological Society

Printed by The Friary Press, Grove Trading Estate, Dorchester.
Published by The Dorset Natural History and Archaeological Society,
Dorset County Museum, Dorchester, Dorset DT1 1XA.
© C. J. Bailey and DNHAS, 1982.

British Library Cataloguing in Publication Data

Bailey, C. J.

    The Bride Valley
    1. Bride Valley (Dorset)—History
    I. Title
    942.3'31   DA670.B/'

    ISBN 0-900341-16-5
    ISBN 0-900341-15-7 Pbk

Cover: The Bride near its source at Little Bredy.

Contents

		Page
	Preface	vii
1.	The natural setting	2
2.	The valley in prehistoric and Roman times	3
3.	Early records	6
4.	The ancient parishes	7
5.	Littlebredy	10
6.	Kingston Russell	19
7.	Longbredy	27
8.	Litton Cheney	46
9.	Chilcombe	62
10.	Puncknowle	67
11.	Bexington	79
12.	Swyre	82
13.	Shipton Gorge	90
14.	The lost village of Sturthill	95
15.	Burton Bradstock	98
16.	Summary	107
17.	Ordnance Survey map (1811)	109
18.	Map references of archaeological sites	110
19.	Summary of Domesday Book returns	111
20.	Bibliography	112

Preface

Over the years it has been my privilege to talk to many and varied audiences about Dorset's past with particular reference to the valley of the River Bride. In so doing I have always tried to relate photographic slides of the present with the story of bygone years. It seemed appropriate therefore, in answer to the many requests for a book on the valley, that the same technique should be used. With a few exceptions the photographs reproduced here were taken by myself in 1981-82 and are laid out, as far as possible, opposite the relevant text.

For much of the archaeological record I have been able to draw on my own work for the Dorset Natural History and Archaeological Society. Local history references from published material have largely had to be drawn from works on the county as a whole. With the general reader in mind a bibliography has been included but specific references have been omitted. The detailed card index of sources both published and unpublished built up during the preparation of this book will be available to the specialist student in the library of the County Museum.

My maps of the villages are based on Isaac Taylor's *Dorset* (1765), the first general map to detail buildings and roads. For comparison the relevant part of the first Ordnance Survey (1811) has been included. I have assumed that the reader unfamiliar with the area will be able to consult modern Ordnance Survey maps.

I am grateful to the farmers and landowners who, without exception, allowed me access to their land to carry out the all-important field-work and to Elizabeth Lady Williams for opportunity to see and make use of the Bridehead papers.

My greatest debt is to the Council of the Dorset Natural History and Archaeological Society which has undertaken this publication on my behalf and I must thank Jo Chaplin, the Editor; Derek Beamish, the Local History Editor; and Roger Peers, the Society's Secretary for their help and advice in its preparation.

The photographs were processed by Peter Wilbourne, Geoff Long and my son Andrew whose wife Eve also prepared the typescript; I owe much to their invaluable assistance. Above all my thanks are due to my wife, Susie, not only for her interest in the book but also for her forebearance over the years when archaeological field-work occupied so much of my spare time.

Longbredy
Dorset   C. J. BAILEY
June 1982

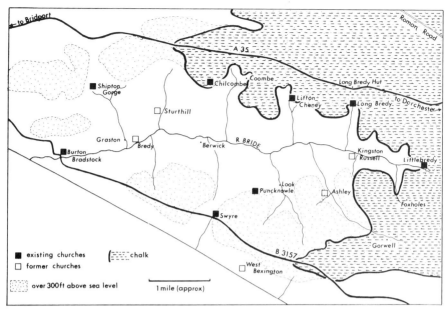

1. The valley today lies between two main roads. The A35 follows an ancient highway but the coast road was not developed till the 1930s.

2. The Bride at Kingston Russell in January 1982.

THE NATURAL SETTING

The dictionary definition of a river as a 'copious stream flowing to the sea' seems hardly appropriate for the little Bride, yet, with nine tributaries along its six and a half mile course from source to mouth, it presents a complete river system in miniature. Moreover, just as Dorset as a whole has landscapes representative of three great geological epochs, so does the 15 square mile catchment area of the Bride.

East of the source at Littlebredy a cap of geologically recent gravel lies over the chalk and forms a small area round Blagdon Hill resembling that of the heathland of East Dorset. It is, in fact, an isolated remnant cut off from the same gravel sheet which once extended much farther to the west.

The chalk hills that form the head of the valley reach westwards along half its length and rise to the great undulating downland that forms the heart of the country. The chalk, and the greensand beneath it, has a steep slope from the base of which the springs which feed the river rise where the water-bearing sand lies against the valley clay.

Just as the chalk, which also extended far to the west, has mostly been removed by erosion from that part of the country, so the floor of the valley has been cut down to the earlier limestones and clays. The limestone hills which flank the western end of the valley are lower and have gentle slopes.

The Bride

Any romance in the name must be at once ruled out. River names are generally far older than place names so that our local forbears – Celtic, Romano-British, Anglo-Saxon and Norman and their descendants no doubt used a word sounding something like 'Bridda'. Place name experts suggest that it originally meant, in the Celtic, gushing or boiling, aptly describing the little stream which falls more than 200 feet in its first three miles.

The earliest documented reference to the Bride is in 1288 when it is referred to as the 'aqua de Brydie' though for the villages of Longbredy and Littlebredy we have 'Bridian' recorded as early as 987. The Domesday Book spelling of Langebride for Longbredy (1086) causes some confusion. It would have been in fact pronounced 'Langabridda'. By the 15th century we have 'Bredy' though it would still have been pronounced to rhyme with 'ready'. That form of the names is used on the 1811 Ordnance Survey Map. It is significant that the old pronunciation is still used by older people with deep roots in the valley who will say 'Longbriddy' rather than the modern 'Longbredy'.

The long 'i' of Bride and the long 'e' of Bredy are relatively modern developments of the word. Indeed Bridehead as a name is no older than 1797 when Robert Williams bought the manor of Littlebredy and as well as rebuilding the house, dammed the nearby source of the stream to form a lake, and surrounded the whole with a landscaped park. The name chosen for the new estate was Bridehead.

THE VALLEY IN PREHISTORIC AND ROMAN TIMES

The Neolithic and Bronze Ages

Where there is no written record our knowledge of man in the past depends largely on the interpretation of the evidence from archaeological excavation. However some of the more substantial results of his activity in prehistory can still be seen. Earthworks such as the long communal burial mounds of the ruling classes of the New Stone Age (about 3500 to 2500 BC), the individual round barrows of the Bronze Age (which lasted for the next 1000 years or so) and the earth and stone circles and field banks have in many cases by their very nature survived; they are a prominent features of the hills around the east end of the valley. The importance of the area in the second and third millenia BC is shown by the fact that the density of barrows north and east of Longbredy and Littlebredy is as high as that round the great prehistoric centre of Stonehenge. In our area, as on Salisbury Plain, they are associated with ritual earthworks and stone circles. Unfortunately we have yet to find their occupation sites. Important monuments still to be seen in the valley area are marked A to G on the map opposite and are illustrated and described in the text under individual parish headings.

Iron Age and Roman Britain

The last half of the first millenium BC saw the establishment of the Celtic Iron Age in Britain. By the time of the Roman Invasion of AD 43 Dorset formed the greater part of the territory of the Durotriges, a tribe whose hill forts are still a feature of the county. Their occupation sites, which rarely have visible remains above ground, are found by intensive field study and/or aerial photography followed in some cases by excavation. Excluding the four fortified enclosures (14-17) the sites numbered on the map were, with a few exceptions, found and followed up (in some cases with excavation) by the writer over many years field work in and around the Bride Valley.

Nearly all were Durotrigian, running on until well into the 4th century AD. The Roman occupation seems to have made little impact on the pattern of rural life in the valley. Burton Freshwater (1), Burton Village (2), Sturthill (4), Higher Coombe (5), Longbredy Village (8), Stonyhills Littlebredy (9), Ox Close Swyre (12) and Greenhill Burton (13) all produced occupation debris typical of the period. The Iron Age/Romano-British farmstead on Pins Knoll, Litton (6) was found and excavated in 1956-60 and the extensive Roman-British site east of Puncknowle in 1965-69. Evidence from the site of the reservoir at Litton raises the possibility of a possible Roman villa in the vicinity and Shipton Hill (14) has produced material from very early in the Iron Age.

The excavated sites are illustrated and discussed here under the relative parishes. More detail can be found in the *Proceedings of the Dorset Natural History and Archaeological Society* wherein all the above sites are recorded.

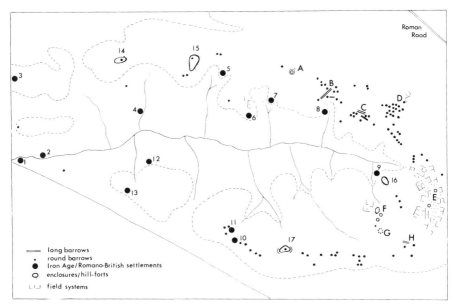

Roman Road

long barrows
round barrows
Iron Age/Romano-British settlements
enclosures/hill-forts
field systems

3. *Prehistoric and Romano-British sites. For precise locations see Appendix A.*

4. *The bank barrow on Martin's Down north of Longbredy Church is the focal point of an important group of prehistoric monuments. The site as a whole is discussed on page 27.* Photo: R. N. R. Peers.

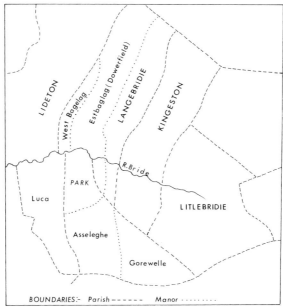

5. *The pattern of the mediæval manors at the east end of the valley is reflected in today's parish and farm boundaries.*

The abbot has 1 manor which is called Langebridia which paid geld in the time of King Edward for 9 hides. Of these the abbot has in desmesne 3 hides and 3 ploughs and the villeins have 5 hides and 1 English thegn has 1 hide. The peasants have 5 ploughs and the thegn has 1 plough. The abbot has 7 villeins and 9 coscets and 3 serfs and 1 pack-horse and 15 pigs and 353 sheep and 20 goats and 1 mill which renders 6s. a year and ½ league of woodland in length and 3 furlongs in width and 11 acres of meadow and 1 league of pasture in length and 1 league of pasture in widthe. This manor renders £16 for the use of abbot and £3 for the use of the thegns.

The return in the Domesday Book for the Abbey of Cerne's Manor at Longbredy.

EARLY RECORDS

The earliest documentary evidence for the valley is dated 987 when the eastern end was part of the Saxon Earldom of Cornwall. It was then that Earl Aethelmaer gave the whole of Littlebredy and part of Longbredy to Cerne Abbey. Longbredy and Littlebredy have always been served by the same priest so that Littlebredy Church was sometimes referred to as a chapel of Longbredy; this suggests that in the very early days the two villages were adjacent to each other. This is substantiated by the fact that the boundary between Kingston Russell and Longbredy has features which point to its being made long after the latter village had become well established, and that what later became the manor of Kingston Russell was originally part of Longbredy. Moreover, when Aethelmaer gave the lands to Cerne, care seems to have been taken to avoid their owning it in one large block. The map opposite shows how Cerne's main manor in Longbredy was separated from that of Littlebredy by a strip retained in royal hands – the King's ton; to the west the main manor was separated from the smaller Baglake by the manor of Dowerfield, likewise kept as crown land. In fact the latter continued to be part of the Duchy of Cornwall right up to the present century.

The lack of records during the next hundred years is made up by the extensive detail of the Domesday Survey of 1086. The Norman conqueror, William, intended to find out accurately the lands and wealth he claimed for himself. The survey was rather like a modern census and income tax demand in one, except that the mostly illiterate population were required to answer orally the list of questions, always put in the same order by the King's Commissioners and the answers were recorded by clerks who even contrived a special shorthand to make the task easier. Their purpose was, as recorded in the Saxon Chronicle, 'to ascertain how much land and livestock the King himself owned in each county and what annual dues were lawfully his from each shire . . . what land his bishops, abbots and earls had and how much each man who was a landowner here, in England, held in land or in livestock and how much money it was worth'.

For the Bride Valley the record is almost complete and shows the village pattern, except for the lost manor of Sterte (Sturthill), much as it is today. Burton, being a royal manor, is grouped with other royal lands outside the valley and is not detailed. Kingston and the royal Dowerfield, being small, may have been hidden in a collective return. Litton was not included as a place name but is very likely a manor merely recorded as belonging to two brothers. There are full entries for the other manors in the valley and they are discussed later under the appropriate village headings.

After the Domesday Survey there is almost complete silence in the documentary record. Not until the middle of the 1200s do we learn much about village history when a fondness for litigation as a way of settling arguments brought about a sudden increase in court records and other legal documents.

THE ANCIENT PARISHES

The parish boundaries as established over 1000 years ago were probably little changed over the first 500 years. The period from 1450-1550, however, saw the decay, over much of the country, of many once-thriving villages and the Bride Valley was no exception.

Bexington had been a village, certainly from well before the 11th century. By 1451 it had suffered so much from poverty and from the raids of French pirates that the Bishop ordered its church of St. Giles to be abandoned. It was further decreed that the parish should be united with Puncknowle which was thus extended to reach the sea.

Of the mediæval village of Sterte (Sturthill) there is today little trace. We know from documentary records that the chapel of St. Luke was served by parsons from 1240 to 1545 when it became so impoverished that the living was left vacant and the few remaining inhabitants had to use Burton Church. Although united with the latter ecclesiastically, physically the parish was divided between Burton and Shipton.

Kingston Russell village, with records from 1280, lost its church at the same time. The village having become so depopulated the cure of souls of those left was transferred to the Rector of Longbredy and its chapel, dedicated to St. James, fell into ruin. The civil parish, however, still remains intact.

As the map shows, Litton (Lideton) was a large parish made up of three distinct parcels. To the north an isolated area, known in parish records as 'Loderland', reach as far as Eggardon Hill; to the south the triangle formed by Parks Farm, Gorwell and Ashley formed another outlier; in the centre was the village and the church. This untidy state of affairs was not to be tolerated by modern civil administration so that when the Local Authorities were set up in 1889 changes were made. Loderland was shared out between Askerswell and Loders, Ashley, Gorwell and Parks Farm were transferred to Longbredy and the central block became the Litton of today.

The ancient manor of Look (Luk), first record 1230, was in fact an outlier of Abbotsbury parish. Until 1889 Abbotsbury thus extended right down into the valley with the Bride as its northern boundary. This anomaly was tidied up by giving Look to Puncknowle and by compensating Abbotsbury with part of the old Bexington manor. This was done by moving the boundary line of Abbotsbury, which originally passed through the hill-fort and down to the sea, further west to pass through Tulks Hill.

It is not known precisely what factors determined the positioning of the parish boundaries. It is at once obvious from the map that use was made of natural as well as man-made landmarks; hills, coombes, streams, hill-forts, barrows and the Roman road all serve a purpose. Moreover the pattern seems to show a fair distribution of land resources. Thus Puncknowle and Swyre, both hill-top villages, have boundaries so contrived to reach and include a length of the river in the valley below. Each could thus have a water-mill which was so vital a part of mediæval village life. The Domesday Survey of 1086 recorded mills for both manors.

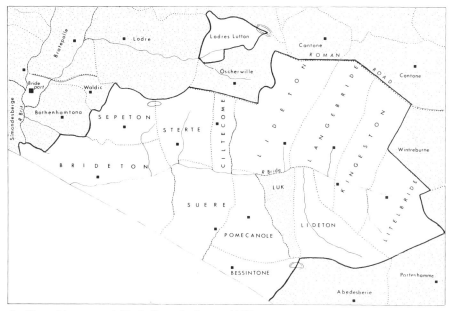

6. The parishes as recorded in the Domesday Survey of 1086.

7. The largest round barrow in the Poor Lot Group and another on the skyline mark Kingston Russell's boundary with Littlebredy and Winterbourne Abbas.

8. *Sarsens and prehistoric field systems in the Valley of Stones. Some of the boulders are more than 10 feet across.*

9. *Old Warren has a commanding position rising some 250 feet above the floor of the valley.*

LITTLEBREDY – ARCHAEOLOGY

The Valley of Stones

The upper length of the Bride Valley, about a mile above Littlebredy, is well known for the many great boulders that are strewn thickly along its floor and litter its slopes. Geologically the stones are the remains of a layer of sands and gravels laid down on the top of the chalk. Exposed to drying conditions when the sea receded they became naturally cemented to form a thin sheet of very hard rock which was subsequently broken up by earth movements and by erosion. These 'sarsens' are thus conglomerates, sometimes of grey sand and pebbles, sometimes of sand and small, angular flints. There is evidence that they were once much more widely distributed over the chalk downland of West Dorset. The Valley of Stones (Fig. 3,E) and its surrounding countryside provided the material for the stone circles and chambered tombs in the neighbourhood, in fact two-thirds of Dorset's monuments of this nature lie within four miles of the valley and the whole area shows intense prehistoric activity. Despite their huge size, they have been cleared from fields over the centuries. Even in the Valley of Stones, where they are most concentrated, some have been removed to one side.

Apart from the use of these stones the main evidence of early activity in the area is the wide distribution of small, squarish fields. Although the word 'Celtic' is generally used to describe them some may, in fact, be earlier than the Celtic Iron Age and many were in use during the Roman Occupation which followed it. While the fields are numerous, the occupation sites which must have been associated with them have left very little trace and their whereabouts is one of the tantalising problems of the archaeology of the area.

Old Warren (Fig. 3, No. 16)

High on the hill which towers above Littlebredy on the south, this earthwork poses yet another problem. Aerial photography and archaeological field work suggests that it was an Iron Age hill-fort with a single rampart. On the other hand historically the Burghal Hidage (a list of Saxon fortifications, set up at the time of King Alfred against the Danes) refers to 'Brydian' as such a stronghold, somewhere between Wareham and Exeter. The same word was used when what is now Littlebredy was granted to Cerne Abbey in 987. Some authorities suggest, therefore, that Old Warren was indeed an Iron Age hill-fort but that it was adapted as a burh or fortified place in the 9th and 10th centuries and later abandoned when the Danish threat had passed. Against this, recent field work, in conjunction with documentary research makes it possible that the Anglo-Saxon town of Bridport was the burh 'in Brydian'. The relationship between the 'Bride' element of the old name Brideport and the name of our river will be discussed later. Whatever its subsequent use, Old Warren almost certainly began as an Iron Age hill-fort. From its foot a greensand spur projects into the valley. On the flattish top of this spur the writer has found evidence of Iron Age/Romano-British occupation (Fig. 3, 9) and the discovery of a burial of that period when the road to Foxholes was made last century is recorded in the Bridehead papers.

LITTLEBREDY – The Mediæval Manor

If the Old Warren site was, in fact, that of Alfred's Burh in Brydian, then our earliest documented date must be around 910 AD. In any case, the manor of Brydian was already established when Aethelmaer gave it to the Abbey of Cerne in 987; a hundred years later the Domesday Survey details the Abbot's holding there. Half the lands of the manor of 'Litelbridia' were farmed by the abbey itself with two ox teams to do the ploughing. The other half was held by the villani (the higher class of peasants) in small, scattered strips. In return for their holdings they would, as well as paying dues in kind, have to work part of the time on the abbey land. Since they, with an almost equal amount of land, had six ox teams, it seems that the abbey concentrated on sheep. In fact Litelbridia carried 550 sheep out of the total 2632 listed as being owned by Cerne on its 17 Dorset manors. Sheep, of course, were then farmed not only for mutton and wool but also for their milk and the cheese made from it.

For the next 200 years life on the manor would have changed little except that gradually the custom of holding by service on the Lord's land gave way to holding by payment of money. The peasants on the lower class levels who held no land could then be paid to work for the lord or for others who were thus privileged.

Two documents referring to transfer of land within the manor in 1287 are of interest. Adam de Corston and Mathia, his wife, are passing their holdings on to their children. Totalling some 80 acres, the land is scattered in small strips throughout the manor; these are identified by naming the holders of the adjacent strips. As would be expected the abbot is named most often together with the land-holding 'villani'. Some of the place names can still be identified though most are long since forgotten:

one acre of land in Voxcumbe (modern Foxholes) near Ralph le Fevre's land on the south;
half an acre at Porta de Pidecumbe (Pitcombe) near Ralph le Strange's land on the west;
one acre in le Breche (Brakes) near Walter Leulin's land on the south;
one acre near Les Hoges on the east (Hoghill).

Apart from these documents we know nothing of Littlebredy while it was held by Cerne. We must suppose that the Abbey Farm was managed by a bailiff who was responsible for seeing that the returns, both in cash and kind, duly found their way to the abbot.

Two ancient trackways leading out of the village, traces of which remain today as hollow-ways, can be identified. 'Bowprest Way' climbed up over the hill to the south of today's cricket pitch and followed the same line as today's bridle path to Abbotsbury. The Alba Via of the document runs virtually up the White Hill of today though this could also refer to another old route out of Littlebredy which ran up the side of the combe north of the lodge on the road to Pitcombe. It, too, is a well defined hollow-way in the chalk; it could very well have been the line of communication between Littlebredy and Cerne.

10. *Cerne Abbey's manor of Litelbridia would have had few trees. Today's parkland was laid out first by Robert Mellor in the 17th century and later by the Williams family.*

11. *The source of the stream at Bridehead. The springs well up beneath the lake and the water cascades over the dam to the original level.*

12. *Bridehead House and lake nestle beneath the hills. As the trees planted last century mature, scars like that on the far slope become inevitable.*

13. *The cottages between the church and the little thatched school (now the village hall) are the only survivors of the Mellors' 17th century estate.*

LITTLEBREDY – From Cerne Abbey To Robert Williams

The situation of Cerne's manor house at Littlebredy is not known but we may reasonably suppose it was on or near the site of the Bridehead of today; nor can the two or three open fields of the manor be located. The hilly nature of the countryside and the very little valley land would suggest that the strips were not, as was usual, in blocks forming the open fields; the wide scatter of Adam de Corston's little plots confirms this. There is abundant evidence of mediæval cultivation as strip lynchets along the south-facing slopes of the chalk hills and in the field systems on the hillsides and in the coombes to the south of the village.

One of the most important assets of the mediæval manor was the mill but none was recorded in the Domesday Survey of Litelbridia nor is there any indication of one in later documents until Taylor's map (1765); he shows it on the river just west of the village. The field to the south of the river is shown as Miller's Mead on the Tithe Map.

We know little of the inhabitants of Littlebredy during the time (more than 500 years) that Cerne held the manor but we do know something of the parsons, thanks to the detailed research of the late Canon F. E. Trotman, one-time rector of the Bredys. He gives Richard de Preston as the first named priest in 1297 and interesting details of the 18 who, in turn, followed him. All were presented by the Abbot of Cerne; the last was Roger Bond who, in 1531, was also appointed to Kingston Russell.

Eight years later Cerne Abbey was dissolved and its lands sold. In 1544 the manor of Littlebredy was bought by Philip Vanwilder who resold it 40 years later to Robert Freke of Iwerne Courtney. Robert settled it on his son-in-law Robert Mellow who moved from Came House to Littlebredy, building the first known house on the present Bridehead site late in the reign of Elizabeth I. Sir John Mellor, who succeeded the first Robert at Littlebredy, was heavily fined for his loyalty to Charles I during the Civil Wars. He bequeathed the manor to his younger son, another Robert, who died at Littlebredy in 1655, but, like all the Mellors, he was buried at Came. His widow bequeathed Littlebredy to her son Edward but he went to live at Chenies at Buckinghamshire, taking the coat of arms which had been in the manor house at Littlebredy with him. Before he died in 1699 he had sold off some of his Dorset property to pay off debts and, according to a note in the Bridehead papers, Littlebredy was also heavily mortgaged. The same note adds that the Bridges family (who must have been tenant farmers during the Mellors' residence) now moved into the old mansion which became a farmhouse. Taylor's map of 1765 differentiates between 'gentlemen's residences' and farmhouses and that at Littlebredy is certainly shown as the latter. The manor had, in fact, been bought in 1730 by William Meech of Charminster; the Bridges, however, remained as tenants during most of the 1700s; they were buried in the churchyard and their memorials are in the church itself.

Seventeen ninety-seven was a momentous year in the Littlebredy story for it was then that John Meech, grandson of William, sold the estate to Robert Williams of Moor Park in Hertfordshire and a new chapter was to begin.

The Williams Family at Bridehead

Robert was descended from an old Dorset family, his grandfather being one of the Williams who had been at Winterbourne Herringston since the reign of Henry VIII. Having gained eminence as a London banker and become the owner of extensive property, as well as of a fleet of ships trading with the Indies, he bought Littlebredy for his country seat and began the slow transformation of the old village into the Bridehead Estate. Slow because three more generations, all Roberts, were to play their part in the development of house, grounds, church and village.

By the 1830s the small Mellor house had been virtually rebuilt and extended westward, the nearby source of the Bride dammed to make a lake and the whole surroundings landscaped. A note among the Bridehead papers suggests that the lake and garden were made following the burning down of the original farm buildings which were to the west of the house. Further additions to the house itself were made in 1850.

At the same time as the house and grounds were developing along lines typical of an estate of the period, changes were made deliberately turning the old village into a model community. Gradually the old cottages of the Mellor Estate were replaced but much thought was given to planning and the old-world charm retained. Even the stables were designed in Gothic style by the noted Victorian architect Benjamin Ferrey; the same buildings today form the nucleus of the estate farm. The two model cottages and detached schoolhouse north of the road were built some years later but the little thatched school (now the village hall) was also the work of Ferrey and matched the adjacent 17th century cottages. Long drives were made connecting Bridehead with the turnpike road, each with lodges. That at Winterbourne Abbas was built in 1837 in a castellated style similar to Bridehead.

In turn the four Roberts, while expanding their estate, played leading parts in the life of the county and county town as well as being Members of Parliament. The last Robert also held executive positions in the Church Missionary Society and in the Church Assembly and became the 1st Baronet of Bridehead.

Life at Littlebredy was, as in so many English villages last century, dominated by the big house and the church. The first Robert had married Jane Chasserau, the daughter of a French refugee, long before coming to Bridehead; her influence in the shaping of their early days there lasted long after her death in 1841 at the age of 102 years. Years later her great granddaughter wrote, 'She was a fine lady and began, I think, the tradition of Bridehead, thank God carried on to this day, of Christian faith and of Christian life and service'.

Since the Mellors had buried at Came, memorials to the Williams family dominate the church and churchyard at Littlebredy. The vault used for their burials in the first part of the last century is on the north side of the church. A note in the Bridehead papers describes how, when walking through the churchyard, Jane saw men making the vault and said to an old man working there, 'Do you know you are digging my grave? You will share my grave – will you also share my salvation?'.

14. *The east front of Bridehead House follows the line of the Mellors' building which was altered and enlarged by the first Robert Williams.*

15. *The site of Cerne Abbey's mediæval farm may well lie beneath the lake created by the early 19th century landscaping.*

16. *Littlebredy Church was rebuilt in 1850. It incorporates part of the mediæval chancel and a spire has been added to the 14th century tower.*

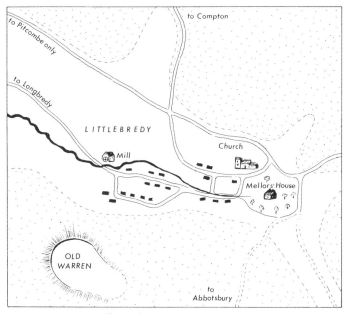

17. *Littlebredy in the early 1700s.*

LITTLEBREDY

The Church of St. Michael and All The Angels

Old illustrations of the church show it as a small nave and chancel with a low tower over the entrance on the south side. The mediæval building was already in a bad state when Robert Williams bought the manor. Some repair was carried out by the second Robert but without much success so that when his son followed him in 1847 he soon set about remodelling the whole building.

Benjamin Ferrey, who was responsible for much church restoration in Dorset, was the designer of the new building but the architect on the site was Robert Williams' brother-in-law, Arthur Acland, who had previously worked with Ferrey. As the Bridehead papers show, the whole exercise caused much stir in the village; a small army of workmen, mostly lodged with the local population, demolished the old building (save for the tower and part of the chancel) and rebuilt it. The chancel was drastically restored but retained some of its mediæval windows: the nave was completely replaced with an extension to the west and north and south aisles were added. The small tower was strengthened to carry a steeple and four new bells brought the peal up to six. Acland and his family lived at Bridehead during the reconstruction and he himself did the carving of some of the interior stonework. The final cost, met by Robert Williams, was almost £1000. The memorials to the Bridge family, placed in the old building in the 18th century, were reset in the south wall of the new nave. Before the nearby parsonage was built the curate lived in a small house at the bottom of the village.

The Village

Taylor's map gives some indication of the plan of the village and its roads as they were when the Williams family first came to Littlebredy. Most of the cottages were in the valley bottom, on the south side of the stream, between the mill on the west and the Mellor mansion (then the Bridges' farmhouse) on the east. It should be remembered that the trees which are a feature of the village today had not then been planted. No buildings are shown north of the church and the main street, like the cottages, ran along the valley bottom eastward to the mill. Having forded the stream the road continued straight on to Kingston Russell. It is shown on both Taylor's map and that of the first Ordnance Survey but no trace of it remains today.

The line of the modern road from Littlebredy to Longbredy which runs via Pitcombe is part of the development of the Bridehead Estate of last century. The old road also left Littlebredy just west of the mill and ran in a more or less straight line to the same point as the present road enters Longbredy; in doing so it by-passed Pitcombe and Kingston Russell House. The only part of it used today is the straight length past Whatcombe House but the original line can partly be traced. Pitcombe originally had its own road from Littlebredy; last century another was made from the farm to join the old road at Ash Tree Gate to the south-west. These two then became part of the main route between the villages, thus accounting for the angles in the present road.

KINGSTON RUSSELL – Prehistory

An ancient trackway runs along the ridge of the chalk hills to the north of the eastern part of the Bride Valley and associated with it is one of the most marked concentrations of prehistoric burial mounds in the country. The Poor Lot Group (Fig. 3,D) is especially important with its 44 barrows representing all types.

In 1971-3 the writer excavated three round barrows at the top of the old road leading out of Kingston Russell. They are shown as the three most westerly of Group C (Fig. 3). The purpose of the excavation, which was carried out by permission of the Department of the Environment, was to rescue information before the mounds were completely destroyed by cultivation.

One of these was a disc barrow (so-called because of its small central mound and encircling bank). They are generally considered to be the monuments to the important women of the warrior aristocracy which ruled Wessex early in the Bronze Age. The grave of this barrow was found to have been re-used four times. The last two crouched burials, both female, were found lying one on top of the other. Two other child burials were also found beneath the mound. Later in the Bronze Age the custom changed to cremation and the mound was found to contain a cremation urn of this period.

The second barrow excavated, although typical in construction (a mound surrounded closely by a ditch), was very unusual in that there was no grave. The crouched body had been laid on its side and a mound of flints raised over it. The third excavation showed a barrow and an associated cremation cemetery. One exception was the crouched burial of a child whose feet had been chopped off.

Tenants Hill

Although the density of barrows is not so great on the chalk to the south of the Bride there is much evidence of prehistoric activity (Fig. 3,F). On Tenants Hill, right in the corner of the parish, is a circle about 80 ft. in diameter, of fallen sarsen stones; the longest is about 8 ft. Such circles are generally dated early in the second millenium BC and thought to have a ritual purpose. A smaller circle on Hampton Down (in Portesham parish) about one and a half miles away was excavated in 1967; no finds were made other than sockets for the stones so that it seems that burials were not associated with these rings.

A little to the north of the Kingston Russell Circle, and perhaps more important archaeologically, is a well preserved settlement site, probably of the later Bronze Age. A roughly oval enclosure of about one-third of an acre is surrounded by a bank and ditch with an entrance on the east. From it another bank runs up the hill to a well defined hut circle. Associated with the settlement are prehistoric field systems which may well be of the same date.

The eastern boundary of Kingston Russell parish is a good example of ancient monuments being used as markers. From the stone circle in the south it runs down into the valley, follows the Foxholes stream to the Bride and then runs north to a barrow on the ridge above Pitcombe, lining up with the largest barrows of the Poor Lot Group.

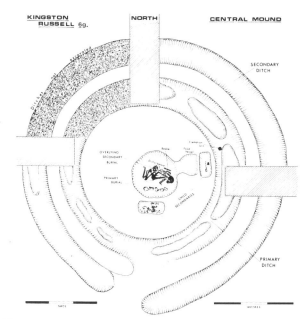

SECONDARY
DITCH

OVERLYING
SECONDARY
BURIAL

PRIMARY
BURIAL

CHILD
SECONDARIES

PRIMARY
DITCH

18.   The plan of the excavation of the disc barrow on the downland north of Kingston Russell House.

19.   The Ministry of Works notice describing the Kingston Russell stone circle proclaims somewhat unnecessarily that admission is free!

20. *The main street of the mediæval village now lies under the garden of Kingston Russell House at the centre of the photograph.*

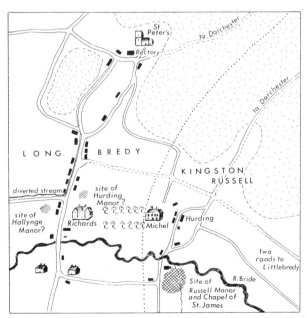

21. *The sites of the few houses remaining in the early 18th century are known from Taylor's map which is corroborated by an estate map among the Bedford papers.*

KINGSTON RUSSELL – The Deserted Village

The name implies a royal manor held after the Conquest by the Norman Russells. There is no record until 1212 when John Russell held it 'of the King'. The same document infers that it seems probable that they took over an already existing Saxon manor. It was held by the ancient custom of serjeanty which required a relatively menial task to be performed annually at the Court, thereby acknowledging the sovereignty of the King. John Russell had to be in attendance from Christmas to Whitsun during which time he had to be 'Marshall of the Buttery' and as such to be in charge of the essential food supplies. When, some 100 years later the Russells had sub-let to the Mortesthorns the service entailed 'counting the King's chessmen and putting them in the box when he has finished playing'.

The manor house must have been on the south side of the river since in 1341, Eleanor Russell was granted one-third of the manor of Kyngeston, Co. Dorset including 'a high chamber towards the chapel'. Today no trace remains except for its fishponds and the humps and hollows which mark the village which grew up around it. In 1281 William Russell was granted full manorial rights at Kingston including a market there on Thursdays and an annual fair on the eve, day and morrow of St. Matthew (Sept. 20th-22nd). Certainly by 1302, and probably before, the village had its own church, the 'free chapel' of St. James. Its site today, close by the stream on the south side, is waterlogged for much of the year and subject to flooding. John Baverstock Knight, the Duke of Bedford's agent in the valley early in the last century, wrote, 'in 1811 the old milking barton was on the site of the Kingston chapel and chapel yard and I recollect seeing a small part, or rather indication of the ruin yet standing to mark the locality, but this inconsiderable vestige of what once had been was all that the oldest inhabitant then remembered'. Dorset historian John Hutchins, almost 100 years before, saw the walls of the old chapel still standing and recorded that within the last 50 years it had been inhabited by poor people. Nothing is left today to mark the site. It may well have been that the wet years of the late C14 hastened the decay of both church and village. A graveyard at river level must have presented problems.

By the beginning of the 15th century the Russells' interest in the place had also begun to decline and when, in 1432, Thomas Russell died leaving no male heir, the manor was divided between his two sisters who had both married into Gloucestershire families. A hundred year later the Russells of Kingston were but a memory in the valley. By then the village had so declined that the church was united with Longbredy and the few remaining inhabitants of Kingston had to bury there. The lands of the manor were sold, the larger part being bought by the second Earl of Bedford; it has been suggested that in so doing he believed he was buying back his ancestral home. The pros and cons of this will be considered later when the Russells of Berwick are discussed.

KINGSTON RUSSELL – From The Michels

Early in the 1600s the Michels, of Dalwood near Axminster, bought part of the former Cerne manor of Longbredy and an adjoining strip of Kingston Russell parish. At the south end of this strip, right on the boundary, they built their first house. Just how it came about that the offices and garden of that house should have been on Bedford land is not clear but the problems which it caused were not solved until an exchange took place in 1769. Almost a century later the Duke was able to buy the whole of the Michel property in Longbredy and Kingston Russell and with it the mansion which, by then, had been substantially altered.

Long before this the Michels had left Kingston Russell for Dewlish and the house had been let. Thomas Masterman was there in 1763 and it was from him that Thomas Masterman Hardy got his christian names. Born at Kingston Russell House on April 15th 1769, the son of Mr. and Mrs. Joseph Hardy, he was later to win fame as the Admiral Hardy of Trafalgar and to be commemorated by the monument which stands on Blackdown, overlooking the head of the valley. Shortly after the house was bought by the Bedfords it was let to Algernon Brinsley Sheridan. His wife was the daughter of the historian John Lethrop Motley who, while USA ambassador to this country, died at Kingston Russell House in 1877. After the Sheridans had left, the house remained unoccupied and soon became derelict. Part of the old east wing was demolished to provide stone for building in Longbredy village. The present Manor Farm House there was built out of it in 1896. The doors and windows of the main block were bricked up so that when sold as part of the Bedford Estate in 1913 Kingston Russell House was virtually in ruins. Undaunted, Mr. George Gribble, who bought it, set about restoration. He took down what was left of the old wing and extended the north and south ends of the main block to give the house its present appearance. The formal yew gardens were also laid out at this time.

During their residence at Kingston Russell the Michels must have found it galling that they could not approach it from the west. Perhaps they, quite early on, anticipated that one day they might do so because they planted a wide avenue of limes in front of the house. Several of these, significant specimens over 300 years old, are still standing. A narrow strip of the other part of Cerne's old manor prevented them from reaching the road through Longbredy village. When, many years later, they were able to buy it, they were no longer interested in making a drive as they had already moved to Dewlish. The present approach road was made by George Gribble in 1914.

The old road from Longbredy to Littlebredy ran much more directly than it does today. Taylor's map of 1765 shows it being crossed by two roads running northwards out of Kingston Russell. The main way out of the mediæval village, the most easterly of the two roads, is still visible today as the hollow-way which is followed up over the down by a bridlepath. The other road, a little to the west, connected the mansion with the valley road and ran on, round the foot of the hill, to Longbredy Church. Some time during the last century new approach roads were made to the north gate of the house; these, today have become the public road which accounts for the acute bend by the gate.

22. *The derelict Kingston Russell House as bought by George Gribble in 1913.*

23. *The east front today showing the 1914 north and south additions. The site of the old east wing lies under the line of trees.*

24. *The site of St. James' Chapel and the Russell Manor House south of the river.*

25. *The line of yew trees marks the line of the mediæval boundary between Longbredy and Kingston Russell.*

The Chapel Of St. James

From Hutchins' description of the ruins it would seem that the chapel was a simple, unpretentious building with no chancel. The first rector to be recorded is about 100 years later than the first reference to the manor.

Fifteen rectors served Kingston Russell from 1308 until 1553. The patrons were the Russells or those to whom they had temporarily leased the manor. Canon F. E. Trotman, in his book *The Rectors of Longbredy in Dorset*, suggests that one of them, Adam Pymer, may well have been an early victim of the Black Death which, reaching Dorset from the continent in 1348, within a few years killed off almost half the population of the country. The consequent breakdown of the finely balanced agricultural economy of the time resulted in the eventual abandonment of many villages; Kingston Russell was one to suffer in this way though other factors may have also been involved.

Not all the rectors would necessarily have lived, or indeed carried out duties, in the village of Kingston Russell. Some held livings elsewhere and the Chapel of St. James, with its rapidly dwindling congregation, may not have been too well served. In 1531 the Abbot of Cerne (the Abbey itself was soon to be broken up) ordered that one priest should serve all three parishes at the east end of the valley and Kingston people use Longbredy Church.

Shortly afterwards the Rectory of Whitchurch Canonicorum held an interest in the glebe and tithes of the chapel. Both Hutchins and Baverstock Knight, writing of Kingston Russell, describe it as 'extra-parochial'. Certainly Whitchurch held some land there in 1549 but no further references are found. In 1739 the tithes were redeemed and the church no longer had any interest in Kingston.

Kingston Russell House

The decay of the mediæval village was already well advanced by the time the Michels built their first house. Certainly it was L-shaped and, most likely in contrast to the present building, had a gabled roof. The east wing, pulled down in 1913, could very well have been part of the original house which was transformed by succeeding generations of Michels.

Around 1675 the east front was rebuilt giving it two ranges of tall mullioned windows; at the same time connecting galleries were added inside to make communications easier in a house which was probably only one room deep.

The early Georgian west front dates from between 1720 and 1739; seven two-windowed bays reach up to the flat roof which is surrounded by a balustrade. A flight of broad steps leads up to the front door with a pediment above.

Both east and west fronts are in Portland stone and retain their original appearance; but when the old wing was pulled down additions were made to the north and south ends, thus spoiling the proportions of the building. Inside the early Georgian staircase remains but the interior decor generally is as it was done for Mr. and Mrs. William Vestey in 1939.

LONGBREDY – Prehistory

Originally in Litton parish but now in Longbredy, close to the boundary with Littlebredy above Gorwell, is an important archaeological monument 'The Grey Mare and her Colts' (Fig. 3,G). Here, some 4500 years ago, use was made of the great sarsens from the nearby Valley of Stones to build a burial chamber of uprights with a capstone. Such tombs were used for collective burials over a period much in the way a family vault is used today. Of the 2000 or so that survive in the British Isles only some 250 are in England and Wales, mostly up the western seaboard. Some of these tombs, as did the Grey Mare, had, in front of the chamber, a forecourt bounded by stones; it is thought that it was used for funeral ceremonies which marked each re-opening of the chamber. Over the whole was built a long mound of earth and stones and this partly remains.

The chamber was opened early last century before the days of systematic archaeology. Little was recorded beyond the fact that it contained many human bones and some pottery. No modern work has been done on the site but it has been suggested that as there are only three uprights the place of the fourth was originally taken by a drystone wall which could be more easily removed to admit further burials.

On the other side of the valley on Martin's Down, to the north of the church at 600 ft. above sea level, is a group of prehistoric monuments centred on the so-called 'Bank Barrow' (Fig. 3, B). The latter is a mound 645 ft. long, 69 ft. wide and 7 ft. high with side ditches; such barrows are rare and virtually confined to Dorset. The Royal Commission on Historical Monuments in its survey of the county, suggests that it has its counterpart in a similar barrow almost 14 miles away in Broadmayne parish; the area between them, with its remarkably high density of barrows, must have had some special significance as the burial place for important folk in the Neolithic and Bronze Ages. Ten round barrows and two long barrows are grouped round the Longbredy Bank Barrow and recently a small 'cursus' has been discovered. Such linear earthworks of two parallel banks and ditches occur elsewhere in association with barrow groups. It has been suggested that they were processional ways most probably associated with funeral ceremonies.

One of the round barrows of the group, by the side of the main road at its junction with the road to North Barn, was excavated in 1964 when the dual carriageway was built. A typical round barrow in form, in use it had similarities with the disc barrow excavated at Kingston Russell in that it had been re-used for burials over hundreds of years and contained the remains of at least six individuals, both adults and children. Similarly the mound had been enlarged by the digging of a second ditch. This ditch contained pottery from the period of the barrow but most of it was of the later Iron Age which had found its way into it while it was still open.

In the valley a short distance from the site of the barrow is a 'standing stone' – an upright sarsen about 7 ft. high, 9 ft. wide and 2 ft. thick. Its association with the bank barrow complex is significant and it may well have had a purpose in religious ritual.

26. *The broken down burial chamber of the long barrow described opposite. The sheep give some idea of the size of the sarsen stones used in its construction.*

27. *The Longbredy Hut round barrow with its flint cairn over the central grave. The dark vertical line in the section in front of the man on the right was cut into the barrow when one of the out-houses of the turnpike inn was built in 1753.*

28. *The regular field pattern running obliquely across the photograph marks the valley strip of Cerne Abbey's manor which lay between Longbredy village and the Kingston Russell boundary.*

29. *Hut Lane marks the line of the ancient boundary between Cerne Abbey's Longbredy manor and the Duchy of Cornwall's Dowerfield. Dowerfield House, tucked under the hill, was not built until early in the 1800s.*

LONGBREDY – The Mediæval Manors

Almost all the village sites in the Bride Valley coincide with those of earlier settlements and at Longbredy 3rd and 4th century Roman coins and pottery have been found, about 400 yards south of the church, by the side of the stream (Fig. 3, 8). The Anglo-Saxon village grew up along the whole length of the stream which flows from the spring near the church down to the river three-quarters of a mile away.

The document which records the gift of land to Cerne Abbey in 987 uses 'Bridian' and 'Further Bridian' for Littlebredy and Longbredy respectively. It may be that 'long' and 'little' were used by the monks to avoid confusion; certainly by the time of Domesday Survey of 1086 they have become Langebridia and Litelbrida.

As we have already seen (page 6) Cerne's Longbredy was split into two by the manor of Dowerfield. It may be that this is the one hide with one plough, held by the English Thegn which was taxed separately in the Domesday Survey. As might be expected, the abbey had more ploughland at Longbredy than at Littlebredy and the home or desmesne farm had three ox-teams for three hides. The word hide originally meant the amount of land required to maintain a free family and its dependents or as much as could be cultivated by one plough in one year. Such a measure was very variable and by the Domesday Survey it referred as much to the potential tax to be collected as to the actual area involved. The 'villani' or villeins at Longbredy had five plough teams between seven of them. A team was made up of eight oxen and could thus be part-shared. There were nine 'coscets' of the cottager class; they would have only been allowed a few acres for their own use and in return would have to work part of the time on the abbey's lands. The few 'servi' were of the lowest class, bondmen of the Lord of the Manor; as such they were little more than slaves.

Cerne's manor of Longbredy was on the east side of the parish between Kingston Russell and the manor of Dowerfield. Its boundary with the latter followed the line of the now vanished Bramble Lane from the Roman Road to Longbredy Hut; it then continued down Hut Lane and round the greensand knoll 'Sands' to the middle of the village. From then on the boundary followed the line of the road down to the river and continued up Abbotsbury Lane to meet the old boundary between Longbredy and Litton.

Between Dowerfield Manor and Litton was Cerne's West Baglake, also called Old Baglake. This was a small manor and its lands remained intact as part of one farm until very recently. Hutchins in 1770 described it as 'a former manor and hamlet now depopulated to a single house'. It is so close to Litton that it is generally regarded as part of that village. The second element of the name means a stream but the first is uncertain. Baglake's boundary on the south was the River Bride. That on the north is uncertain but it is unlikely that it reached as far as the Roman Road.

We know very little of the inhabitants of Longbredy during the 500 years when Cerne held most of the parish. As will be seen later, thanks to the researches of Canon Trotman, we do know something of the rectors from 1300 to 1500.

LONGBREDY – The Hurdings

Cerne's Longbredy Manor was sold by the Crown in 1539; Hugh Sidway of Netherbury, who bought it, later divided and resold it. Records show a confusion of dates relating to the various landholders during the reign of Elizabeth I including Thomas Martin (his name continues in 'Martin's Down'), William Prowte of Litton, John Hodder (also of Litton where Hodder's Hill and Hodder's Copse still bear his name) and Henry Hurding.

The Hurdings had farmed land in the valley as tenants of Cerne Abbey since the 1300s. By the time of Elizabeth they had become owners of some consequence, 'Ralphe Hurdinge of Longbriddie' being one of the Dorset 'gentlemen' who contributed to the Armada expenses. By the 17th century their lands included part of the manor of Litton. Although principal landowners they did not hold the right to present the parson to Longbredy Church (that belonged to the Mellors of Littlebredy) but they seem to have been accepted as Lords of the Manor. Their 'mansion' was on the east side of the road at the bottom of the village, just north of the present drive to Kingston Russell House.

The last male of the family, John, died in 1695 and was buried, as were his forbears, in the north transept of Longbredy Church.

The Richards Family

The Hurding property in Longbredy was bought by George Richards, brother of John Richards of Warmwell; both were in business as merchants and importers, chiefly dealing with Spain. The family built 'a handsome red brick house' to replace the old Hurding mansion. According to Hutchins this was in 1740 but there is no doubt that George was living in Longbredy before 1718 as John's still existing account book of 1713-1718 frequently lists merchandise, including foodstuffs and wine, he had bought for him in London to be forwarded to Longbredy; moreover a note in the Longbredy marriage register gives the date of the house as 1709. George was Sheriff of Dorset in 1710 and must certainly have been resident in the county. If Hutchins is correct and it was his son who built the house in 1740 then George senior must have already been living elsewhere in Longbredy, perhaps in the old Hurding house. The second George, having succeeded his father, bought the living of Litton Church to which he presented his son John. The Rev. John Richards, MA, continued to live at Longbredy where for 30 years he was known as the hunting parson. He had his own pack of hounds which he kept not far from the house; a nearby field is still called 'Kennel Mead'.

The red brick mansion, right in line with the front of Kingston Russell House, must have been a constant eyesore. So much so that when John died in 1802 leaving no son the Michels took the opportunity of buying the estate and completely demolishing the house without trace! Some years later they converted the stables of the Richards' house into a farmhouse (now the home of the writer). The high wall round its garden was built from the bricks of demolished mansion and it has, over the front door, an oval window which almost certainly came from the red brick house, the foundations of which were exposed when the drive was recently extended.

The Richards family are, like some of the Hurdings before them, buried in the north transept of Longbredy Church.

30.　The site of George Richards' mansion. Its existence was brief – less than 100 years. The photograph is taken through the oval window below.

31.　Having demolished the Richards' house the Michels converted its stables into a farmhouse. The oval window from the mansion was inserted over the doorway of the stables which still carries its 1706 date-stone.

32. *All the 19th century Bedford Estate houses are on the east side of the street and stream, i.e. on Cerne Abbey's mediæval boundary.*

33. *Modern building has moved the village further down into the valley leaving the old rectory (c. 1770), the old school and schoolhouse (1855) and the church as an isolated group.*

LONGBREDY – From 1800

Having bought the Richards estate to add to the land they already held in Longbredy the Michels were now the owners of the whole of the old manor. Their chief tenant was Joseph Symes who lived in Kingston farmhouse and leased 1100 acres from them. The open lands north of the main road, much of it common, had been enclosed by 1600; out of them two farms had been created with houses only a few hundred years apart – the Michels' Kingston Farm on the Longbredy side with the Bedfords' Kingston Russell Farm just over the boundary.

In 1862 the whole of the Michel property was bought by the Bedford Estate including Kingston Russell House. The then Duke was always concerned for the living conditions of his tenants and by the end of the century the village of Longbredy had been largely rebuilt. The semi-detached houses which line the street and stream were completed between 1865 and 1868. What is now Manor Farmhouse was built in 1890 using stone from the then partly demolished east wing of Kingston Russell House. The estate also extended the farmhouse built by the Michels out of the old Richards' stables and added a set of farm buildings.

The Bedford ownership was relatively short for in 1913 they sold all that they had bought from the Michels in 1862. Out of the sale two small family farms were created but the bulk of the property was still to belong to one owner. As we have seen the Gribbles bought Kingston Russell House, and with it went 124 acres partly in Longbredy and partly in Kingston Russell. Alfred Symes, the sitting tenant, bought the 790 acres which extended from the Roman Road, through Kingston Farm, right down to the church. This he sold shortly afterwards to the Gribbles' eldest son, Philip. He lived at Piddletrenthide Manor and put a bailiff into Kingston Farm to manage both his own and his parents' land.

With Kingston Russell House the senior Gribbles had acquired the farmhouse built by the Michels on the site of the Richards' stables. This unit, at the end of the newly-made drive to the house, they developed as offices, garage and kitchen gardens. The whole gave considerable employment locally. The hall by the farmhouse was built in memory of Julian Gribble, VC, who died a prisoner-of-war on Armistice Day 1918.

The Gribbles' interest in Longbredy was even shorter than that of the Duke of Bedford; it began to decline with the death of Mrs. Gribble in 1923 and ended with that of her husband in 1927. In the meantime Philip Gribble had sold Kingston Farm. Kingston Russell House and its 124 acres were sold in 1929. Another change of ownership divorced the house (which was bought by Mr. and Mrs. William Vestey) from the land which after being farmed separately for some years, was sold and became part of the adjacent Manor Farm.

Today the former Cerne Abbey's manor is divided among five owner-occupied family farms with no single dominating unit.

Longbredy Church

Dedicated to St. Peter it is the most northerly building of the village and almost hidden by hills on three sides. The chancel is unusual in that its roof is higher than that of the nave; it was restored sympathetically by Canon Lundy Foot in 1842 with Benjamin Ferrey as architect. The character of the 13th century original was preserved as were the windows of the same period which are little altered.

As so often happened the parson having restored the chancel (for which by custom he was responsible), the people soon followed and, in 1862/3, helped financially by the Duke of Bedford, rebuilt all the rest of the building except the 15th century tower. The old nave, north transept and south porch were demolished as was the small south transept which had been built by the Michels over their family vault. The arch of the vault can still be seen springing from ground level at the base of the wall of the south aisle. The architect was John Hicks of Dorchester whose 'restoration' removed all trace of earlier construction.

The records of the Diocese of Salisbury record Richard Preston as parson in 1297 but there would have been others before whose names are unknown. A detailed study of the *Rectors of Longbredy in Dorset* was made by Canon E. F. Trotman who was rector here from 1927-47. William Ekerdon 1398-1413 was acquainted with Chaucer, and Canon Trotman liked to think the poet came to Longbredy to visit him. Ralph Ironside (1628-1683) who is buried under the chancel floor, was deprived of his living under the Commonwealth but returned to Longbredy at the Restoration. William Burroughs, who held the living from 1762 to 1790 built himself a new parsonage house; it still stands little changed save for an uncharacteristic colour wash. It replaced a little thatched rectory which stood just to the east with its garden, orchard and 34 acres of glebe. Canon Lundy Foot, who was largely responsible for the restoration of the church, was rector for 44 years and is buried on the left of the path leading to the south porch. William Burroughs' house suffered the fate of so many Georgian rectories this century, and was sold off around 1930. It was replaced with a new one at the bottom of Hut Lane which looked more like a suburban villa than a parsonage house. With the amalgamation of livings, that too has now been sold.

Illustrations of the church before restoration show the Michel aisle with steps leading up to its private entrance. When the north aisle was rebuilt the memorial to John Richards was reset in the west wall. At the same time the broken remains of a monument to John Hurding (died 1677) were found under the floor. The inscribed part was intact and reset in the north wall of the new transept while the broken coat of arms of the Hurding family was built into the wall of the new vestry.

The burial certificate of Anne Richards, wife of George, who died in 1722, was accompanied by an affidavit made before Tho. Pope, Rector of Litton Cheney which read, 'Anne Haine, of the parish of Longbredy maketh oath that the body of Mrs. Anne Richards . . . was buried in woollen according to the true intent and direction of the Act of Parliament for burying in woollen'.

34. The church today is unchanged from the 1870 restoration when the south aisle was added.

35. John Baverstock Knight's painting early last century shows the structure over the Michel vault which preceded the south aisle. The larger house on the right is probably the former rectory. The old road to Dorchester climbing over the hill was in regular use until the beginning of this century.

36. *The harrowed field left of centre is the likely site of the 15th century house of the Hallynges manor which was later known as Hallams Court or Longbridy Farm. The field still called Holland Court is some 300 yards to the north.*

37. *The present Dowerfield Farm (centre) probably corresponds with the old East Baglake which was also known as Dowerfield.*

Dowerfield Manor

The narrow strip separating Cerne's manors in Longbredy had various names, As part of a group of Duchy of Cornwall manors it was known as Ryme Extrinsicus (Ryme without) to distinguished it from Ryme Intrinseca (Ryme within), a parish still so named near Sherborne. Another name was East Baglake. Records show that Dowerfield was held by a succession of families during the 12th and 13th centuries. All, Osbert, Simon and Adam, were linked by marriage and described themselves as 'de Longbredy'. The de Londons followed and they and their neighbour the Abbot of Cerne had frequent disputes which they took to court.

By the 15th century it was held by the Darells and it seems to have then been divided. An inquest as to the possessions of Elizabeth Darell at her death in 1464 showed that she held 'a manor called Hallynges manor in the town of Langebredy and 200 acres of land in Estbaggelake juxta (next to) Langepreddy'. By the time of Elizabeth I the latter was also called Dowerfield and held, in turn, by the Prowtes and Hodders of Litton. A series of leases between 1650 and 1750 relating to Crown lands refer to the manor as a whole as 'Halhams Court alias Longbridy Farm and East Baglake alias Dowerfield'.

Two fields in Longbredy village, on the west side of the stream, are still called Holland Court, a name derived from Halhams Court. When the Rev. John Foote wrote his note in the Longbredy marriage register in 1810 about the Richards' house at the bottom of the village he added, 'Tradition says that a very fine mansion stood formerly in a field near the house, called Holland Court'. This tradition, the site on the Duchy side of the manor boundary, the remains of fishponds that can still be traced and, above all, the diversion of the stream at this point suggest that this was the site of the Halham Court manor house.

There is some evidence that the East Baglake or Dowerfield part of the manor had its house on the site of the present Dowerfield Farm buildings. Some old walling was still visible there within living memory. Moreover early maps show a road leading straight to it from the centre of Longbredy village; the line of this road still shows as a hollow way at the Longbredy end of the footpath to Litton Cheney.

The whole of the Duchy manor was eventually held by the Michels; for a time they owned the neighbouring West Baglake and thus, at the height of their owning land in the valley, they held the whole of the parish of Longbredy.

In the 19th century, with the enclosure of the open downland of the Dowerfield Manor to the north of the Turnpike Road, a farm was developed on the site of today's North Barn Farm. The farmhouse was built away from the farm buildings in the coomb below Longbredy Hut. Today the Crown no longer hold the land, North Barn Farm has its modern house in the valley north of the main road and Dowerfield House has become a private residence. North Barn thus takes its place with Kingston Farm and Kingston Russell Farm; all three are in fact in the upper valley of the Winterbourne. Further south in the Bride Valley the Dowerfield land is shared by three smallholders as tenants of the Dorset County Council who purchased the land from the Duchy.

Baglake

In mediæval times the Abbot of Cerne's small manor of Baglake lay between the Duchy of Cornwall's Dowerfield and the parish of Litton. In early records it is sometimes called West Baglake (to distinguish it from the Duchy's East Baglake) and, more rarely Old Baglake. As with the Longbredy Manor there are very few records of Cerne's tenants.

When the Monastery was dissolved in 1539 Baglake was granted to Sir William Petre and John Kyme. Twenty years later it was resold to 'James Napper of Swyar, yeoman'. The Nappers or Napiers had come to the valley when James' father had married Anne Russell of Berwick and it was he who bought Baglake for his son John. John built himself the house where, 80 years later his great grandson, another John died. He had no heir and Baglake passed to the Napiers of More Crichel who sold it to the Michels of Kingston Russell. They must have allowed the house to deteriorate because, soon after the Lights bought it from them early in the 18th century, it was rebuilt. The William Light initials can still be seen over the archway between the road and the orchard. Which William they stand for is not clear but the last made his home at Baglake. He is buried in Longbredy Churchyard with his wife and two of his seven children. His death (he committed suicide in the pond near the house after a day hunting) was reputed, by tradition, to have been the cause of ghostly appearances and noises at Baglake. The spirit was also said to have been exorcised by a group of clergy who went there for the purpose. They succeeded in confining the ghost to a certain chimney in the house for a number of years when the noises recurred and were considered likely to do so as long as the house should stand.

William's death had occurred in 1749 and by 1790 the Lights no longer held Baglake. During much of the last century and on into this, it was farmed by the Fry family. After the death of the last owner, Robin Wordsworth, the manor, having remained intact for the best part of 1000 years, was broken up.

Longbredy Hut

The name is still given to the junction of the road running north from Longbredy with the A35. In the middle of the 18th century the Turnpike Trusts were set up to meet the need of improved roads for the increasing coach traffic. The Harnham Trust covered the road from Axminster, through Dorchester and Blandford, to Harnham Bridge over the Avon in Salisbury. To pay for the improved road, tolls were extracted from the users. The Longbredy Hut was an inn built in 1753 alongside the tollgate. The first holder of the licence was Elisabeth Crofts, a widow, and the inn continued in use till 1879 when George Saunders was landlord. The growth of the railways greatly reduced the road traffic and the Harnham Trust having expired, the tollgate was removed and the inn demolished. Parts of the foundations were found when the nearby barrow was excavated in 1964. The inn well, which, in spite of its hilltop position, was reputed to always have plenty of water, was found when the new road was made; it now lies filled with concrete under the eastbound carriageway. The stables and garden were on the south side of the road opposite the inn and part of the garden wall was still standing in the 1930s.

38.   *The south block of Baglake House was added by William Light to the older Napier building, traces of which still remain.*

39.   *The Longbredy Hut Inn with its tollgate was strategically placed on the narrow ridge between the Bride and Winterbourne valleys. Its site has been found just to the left of the trees.*

40. *The western gable of St. Luke's chapel. The crude buttressing of the late 1920s can be clearly seen. The Milne-Watson graves are marked with stone slabs and a wall memorial plaque has been recently added. The altar and crucifix were erected by Lady Milne-Watson.*

41. *Ashley Chase lies hidden by a picturesque wooded landscape. The photograph was taken with a telephoto lens from a hill to the south-east.*

ASHLEY – The Chapel in The Wood

The Dorset historian John Hutchins, who was for some time Rector of Swyre, described Ashley in the mid-18th century as 'a farm of whose ancient condition or lords we have no account' which was granted to Sir William Paulet in 1557, adding briefly 'here was a chapel dedicated to St. Luke'. Ashley, until 1899, was part of Litton parish and it was while the writer was searching the records of the mediæval deer park there that the early history of Ashley came to light.

In 1302 Ralph de Gorges, then Lord of the Manor of Litton, was challenged in court by the Abbot of Lettle (Netley near Southampton) to prove the right to land in Ashley. Ralph insisted that it, being adjacent to his park at Litton, had always been in his family. The Abbot, however, was able to show by deed dated 25th June 1246, that William of Litton (Ralph's predecessor) had given the land to the monks of Netley in return for their perpetual prayers for himself and his family. William must have given the land soon after the founding of the Cistercian abbey by Henry III in 1239. Certainly from 1246 till the dissolution of the monastery in 1538 it was held by Netley, probably as a 'grange' or farm run as a community by monks or lay brethren. Ashley's remoteness would have well suited the Cistercian love of seclusion. In 1338 the Abbot had to sue William Gurle, clerk, to render an account while he was bailiff at Ashley.

It is likely that the chapel was built on the slope hard by the farm for the use of the community, and, being deserted when the monastery was dissolved, soon fell into decay. The abbey and its land were in fact bought by Sir William Paulet who thus acquired Ashley some 20 years before the date given by Hutchins.

Today only the western gable end of the small mediæval building survives. It retains its window opening but this has been enlarged to give the impression of a doorway. Sir David and Lady Milne-Watson who bought the farm and built the nearby house in 1925 had a great love for the chapel and lie buried there. To prevent the gable end from falling, one of the stonemasons working on the house was employed to strengthen it. He did this without professional advice so that, while it was saved from falling, the resulting architecture was somewhat bizarre. Years later, in a letter to the writer, he described how he used stone from the bed of the stream to buttress the arch and how, when digging a hole for scaffolding, he found a skull – perhaps of a member of the Cistercian community.

The Paulets soon sold off Ashley and its story thereafter is very much bound up with Litton. The Hurdings owned it in 1657 as part of their 1250-acre estate in the valley. From them it passed to the Richards family and then to the Sheridans.

The word 'chase' has become associated with the woodland at Ashley but in fact is no earlier than the house which was so named by the Milne-Watsons. The building, to the plans of Sir Guy Dawber, has mellowed to blend harmoniously with its landscaped garden and the woods beyond. Only later in the day, when the light falls on the west front, is the natural camouflage ineffective.

Gorwell

The name has changed little from the Old English which meant 'dirty spring'. Like its neighbour Ashley, the manor was in the ancient ecclesiastical parish of Litton. The earliest reference is dated 1285 when 'Ralph Wake holds Gorwell and it belongs to Litton'. Ralph was one of the Wakes who gave their name to Stoke Wake and Caundle Wake in the north of the county. They, or their tenants, were there until 1361 and from then on Gorwell changed hands many times. The Daubneys lived there in the 1500s and George, who died in 1612, has a fine memorial in the chancel of Litton Church. Subsequent owners of local interest include the Chilcotts of Bredy and from them it passed by marriage to George Richards of Longbredy. In 1813 it was leased to William Symonds.

The Wakes had a deer park at Gorwell. In 1361 the manor included '23 acres of meadow within the manor of Litton, and a park, held of Walter Waleys, clerk, by knight's service, in which there are four acres of underwood and herbage worth 13/4d.'. The park, we suspect, was about 85 acres in a triangle bounded by lines running east and north-east from the farm and along the parish boundary with Littlebredy. Memory of it is still retained in the names Park Mead and Park Coppice.

Park's Farm

This farm occupies much of what was once the mediæval deer park of the manor of Litton. Such parks not only provided hunting but also helped fill the Lord's larder with venison. The park 'pale' with its bank, fence and ditch prevented the deer breaking out; it did not, however, prevent poachers from breaking in. The ancient court records are especially helpful in establishing the manor park. Thus the Patent Rolls for 1304 refer to a case on complaint of Ralph de Gorges that 'Nicholas de Maundevill, Geoffrey le Harpour and Henry de Combe, with others, broke his park, hunted therein and carried away his deer'. No doubt Henry provided the local knowledge necessary for the trespass!

Another court action, this time between Ralph and the Abbot of Netley in 1320, was over the possession of Ashley. It proves that the park was already in existence when Ralph's grandfather became Lord of Litton in 1253: 'The Abbot says that a certain William de Lideton, formerly Lord of the Manor of Litton, which is now the manor of Ralph and Alianora de Gorges, gave to the Abbey of Netley all his land in Assheleghe . . . and all the Long Grove up to his park, which is now the park of Ralph and Alianora'. The Long Grove is still there today as 'Long Coppice'; the bank of the park pale is well preserved within the wood and can be traced to the road near Ash Bed. Elsewhere it has been destroyed by cultivation. It showed clearly on an air photograph taken in 1947 and was traced by the writer on the ground in the 1950s. As the map shows it has not been possible to trace it between Ash Bed and Rowden Bridge. Now the area is dairy pasture but within living memory the fields were dotted with oaks, and mature trees are still a feature of the lanesides. They may well be the descendants of those in Ralph's park 600 years ago.

42. *Gorwell Farm lies at the head of a valley through which flows one of the Bride's main tributaries.*

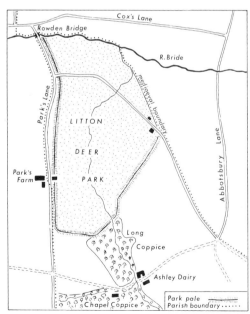

43. *Ralph de Gorge's 13th century deer park lay in the parish of Litton between the Bride on the north and the Netley Abbey's manor of Ashley on the south. It is shown as surveyed in 1958. It is now in Longbredy parish.*

44. A burial of the 1st century AD, one of several in the Durotrigian tradition found on Pins Knoll. Grave goods include part of a sheep as well as the usual food vessel.

45. The walls of a late Romano-British building overlie the Durotrigian corn-storage pits of the pre-Roman period.

LITTON CHENEY – Prehistoric and Roman

West of Longbredy Hut round barrows are relatively few but there is some evidence of a centre of prehistoric activity north of the A35 road above Litton Cheney (Fig. 3, A). Here was an earthwork in the form of an embanked enclosure, thought to have been a henge or ritual monument. However, excavation in 1974 suggested a late Neolithic farmstead later used as a Bronze Age cemetery.

It was the discovery of the Iron Age/Romano-British site on Pins Knoll, west of the village which led the writer to search for other sites in the Bride Valley (page 3). Pins Knoll is a flat-topped spur which juts out into the valley (Fig. 3, 6). At the foot of the hill is a spring; the finding of pottery around this was the first indication of settlement in the vicinity. No surface features of the farmstead remain as the site was very much ploughed in mediæval times, building up the lynchets which can still be seen.

The excavation showed that the settlement had been made up of a small group of huts with more or less continuous occupation over nearly 1000 years. Several thousand pottery sherds were found ranging from the red-coated wares of the first iron-using people, through the typical black vessels of the Durotriges to the black burnished coarse ware and fine imported pottery of the Roman period.

From the 'finds' we can deduce something of the way of life of the people of Pins Knoll. They were farmers growing corn in the squarish field, traces of which still remain on the hill above the knoll. A corn-drying oven was found in which the grain would have been parched before being stored in pits. A number of these pits were excavated and in one many grains of carbonised wheat were found. Such pits, when no longer used for storage, became the equivalent of the modern dustbin; when excavated they often provide the archaeologist with clues and Pins Knoll was no exception. The pig (pork was a favourite meat with the Celts) was much in evidence as well as sheep, goats and a few cattle. Stone loom weights were found; these would have kept the warp threads tight when weaving. Sling stones (carefully selected pebbles) show that they went down to the sea. The most extraordinary evidence of their beachcombing was the finding of the vertebra of a whale in one of the pits! The influence of the Roman Occupation on the lives of the community was shown by the presence of Roman coins, pottery and brooches.

The round huts of the Iron Age folk were followed in the mid-4th century by at least one rectangular building with crude stone walls and a floor of stone slabs. The main source of the stone was the deposits of Corallian Limestone down in the valley but there were a few dressed and squared blocks of Portland Stone which must have come from an earlier sophisticated Roman building not far away. Down in the modern village the writer has found evidence of a possible site for this – east of the church somewhere in the vicinity of Barges Farm (Fig. 3, 7). The position would have been ideal and it may very well be that here part of the present village overlies the site of a Roman villa.

LITTON – Before the Cheneys

The manor is not named in the Domesday record but it must certainly have been well established by then and may well be the unnamed manor of 10 hides in the Hundred Uggescombe, listed under the lands of Hugo de Boscherbert. The name most probably has its origin in the Old English 'hlyde' meaning a fast running stream and 'ton' a farm or manor. Thus we have the spelling Lideton or Ludeton by the 13th century and 100 years later these have become Litton and Ludeton.

At this time the manor was held by the Norman family of de Gorges as part of the greater manor of Chuton (now Chewton Mendip in Somerset) which was held by the overlord Hugh de Vivonia. Near Chuton there was (and still is) another but smaller manor of Litton and this was why, to avoid confusion, our village was often referred to as Great Ludeton in the 13th century. The de Gorges came from Gorges in Normandy: there is still a village of that name about 30 miles south of Cherbourg. Under Henry III, a Thomas de Gorges was made warden of Powerstock Castle and just before his death in 1236 his younger son (both were Ralphs) had purchased the manor of Litton.

For the next 100 years or so Ralph and his heirs held Litton and it seems from the many 13th century lawsuits relating to the manor that they probably lived there. The manor house was most likely where Court House is today. Nearby the banks of its fishponds can still be seen in Court Close: was it from those ponds that Thomas, the parson of Puncknowle, poached Ralph's fish so that he was taken to court in 1267? We have already seen (page 43) that his deer park was a source of attraction for poachers of larger game.

Four generations of Ralphs were to hold the manor of Litton although they also had lands elsewhere, including Bradpole. The fact that Thomas's elder son, also a Ralph, started another family line, whose possessions were to include Shipton Gorge, adds to the confusion of the picture. In 1304 the grandson of Ralph the younger was granted a weekly market at the manor of Lideton, Co. Dorset and a yearly fair there on the Virgil and Feast of the Nativity and six days following (7th-14th September). In 1316 the manor is referred to as Lutton Gorge. All the Ralphs were much involved in the war with France and were knighted for their services.

The last Ralph, the second Lord Gorges, died before 1339 leaving no son and the lands held by him were divided among his three sisters, Elizabeth, Alianora and Joan. Elizabeth, the second eldest, had Litton as her share; she had married Robert de Assheton and when their son, Sir Robert de Assheton, died without an heir, the lands and advowson of Litton which had been allocated to his mother, were also divided. One part went to Alianora's grandson, Sir Morys Russell of Kingston Russell, the other to Robert's cousin Sir Ralph Cheney, the son of Joan, who had married Sir William Cheney. They agreed to share alternately the advowson of the church but Sir Ralph became the owner of the demesne manor and from then on it was Litton Cheney – it could have so easily been Litton Russell!

46. *St. Mary's Church at Litton overlooks the east end of the valley. The field in the centre marks the site of the mediæval fishponds and the manor house. Today's Court House (right) is on the site of the 17th century Hurding manor house.*

47. *The village follows its stream down to the Bride. The parish once extended to Gorwell some three miles away beyond the skyline. The site of the deer park is in the middle distance.*

48. *The division of the manor in the 14th century created a second land unit in Litton. Today's Charity Farm may well be its successor. Parts of the present house date back to the 1600s.*

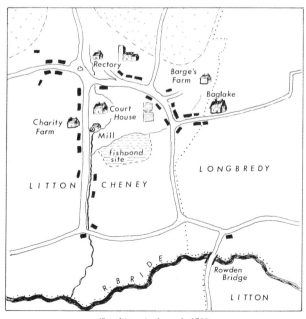

49. *Litton in the early 1700s.*

LITTON – The Divided Manor

The continuation of the Cheney element of the name is surprising since that family only held their part of the Gorges manor for two generations. Sir Edmund Cheyne, the son of Sir Ralph, died in 1430 without a male heir and the Cheney part of Litton passed to his nephew Thomas Russell of Kingston Russell. Thomas was the great grandson of Alianora who had received the other moiety or part of the Gorges' manor and so for a time the whole of Litton was held by the Russells. But, as we have already seen when considering Kingston, Thomas was also last of his line and his property in the Bride Valley came to John Kemys, his brother-in-law, who was more interested in his estates in Gloucester. At some time in the later 15th or early 16th centuries Litton, once more divided, was sold, though to whom and exactly when it not known since the records for this period are very few.

There was a tradition in Litton, which persisted until well into the last century, that the old Court House had once been occupied by a detachment of monks from Abbotsbury who supplied the monastery with fish from the two large ponds nearby. This must have been before 1539. Near these ponds there remain traces of smaller ones used for breeding – in fact, in line with the tradition, a likely fish farm.

When the story of the manor can be taken up during the reign of Elizabeth, the old division of the Gorges manor is still evident. The Prowtes (also of Dowerfield) are in occupation of the farm and manor house; the other lands are held by the Hodders and the Hurdings between them. By the end of the 16th century, however, it is the Hurdings who have become the principal landowners and taken over the manor from the Prowtes. They, as we have seen, lived at Longbredy and let the house at Litton; the Court Books, from 1571 and 1704, show the Hurdings as Lords but the courts are held by the various tenants.

In 1712 the Hurding property in Litton was bought by George Richards of Longbredy. With the manor went the right to present to the church and so his grandson became parson of Litton. With the death of the Rev. John Richards in 1803 the whole of the Richards' property in the valley was sold. Litton was bought to be divided up into smaller units and resold creating new farms. The manor was now reduced to 130 acres and this, together with the rights and privileges that went with it, was bought by the Rev. James Cox. He, and his son after him, both rectors at Litton, were also the last traditional Lords of the Manor.

At this time, the Court House went with Court Farm which had been formed out of the old manor lands. Job Legg who, at the end of the 1700s, was tenant of it under the Richards family, bought 370 acres and with them the old Court House. Today's Court House was built by one of his descendants, Benjamin Legg, on the site of the old house which was destroyed by fire around 1860.

Over the last 100 years the present pattern of farms in Litton has evolved with much changing of owners and redistribution of fields so that today there is no dominant landowner.

LITTON – The Village (1)

The general growth was southwards from the church on either side of the stream and eastwards to the boundary with Baglake. We know that Ralph Cheney's manor was farmed on a three-field system and one of these was almost certainly the rectangular area between the roads south of the church which is now crossed by School Lane. Today's fields, mostly small closes, are typical of an enclosure pattern. Ralph's other open fields were probably the North Field in the 'bottom' north-west of the church with its imposing lynchet system and the East Field, again with lynchets, between Whiteway and the boundary with Baglake.

Although by the 18th century much of the land north of the highroad had been enclosed some, including Litton Common, was divided up into fields by an Enclosure Act of 1812. It was then that the road from the top of Whiteway to the Roman Road was made; the first straight length was entirely new, the second ran along the old road from Longbredy Hut to Eggardon. The wide verges are typical of enclosure roads as they were intended to allow animals to be driven from field to field.

Near the main road and the top of Whiteway is a field called Poor Lot. It was given to the parish when the common was enclosed, as compensation for the loss of the age-old right to gather furze for fuel. The income derived from the letting of the field was, and still is, used to provide fuel for the poor of the parish though today the beneficiaries are mainly pensioners.

Not until the enclosure of the common did Whiteway, with its one in four gradient, become a general route north from the village. The ancient route ran as a continuation of the road from the White Horse, up Watery Lane and then climbed to the main road round the western side of the hill above the church. Part of its course still shows as a hollow-way in the chalk. Crossing the main road diagonally, it followed the line of the parish boundary to the Roman Road and then ran on to Wynford Eagle.

Another 'recent' road is that from Longbredy Lane to Look Farm; before it was made early in the last century, the way from Litton was by Rowden Bridge (there was a cottage on the corner), up the road to Parks Farm and then across to Look by a road which is now lost.

The diversion of the stream round the back of the Court House was probably an early mediæval feature enabling the mill to have a good head of water. The present mill (19th century) is probably the last in a succession on the same site. It was used until the 1930s and some of the machinery and the wheel have been preserved. In fact the Hurdings had two 'water corn mills' in Litton.

The main fishpond, now drained, is still to be seen east of the mill. It was fed by the small stream which rises near the boundary with Baglake. The banks generally are still intact so that only a little building up (at the point where cutting was made to drain it) would be necessary to reinstate this mediæval feature of Litton.

50. *Strip-lynchets north-west of the church formed by centuries of ploughing along the steep slopes.*

51. *The cows are standing in the now dry mediæval fishpond. The stream which originally ran into it has been diverted along the hedge in the foreground.*

52. *A 19th century building took the place of the Poor House which was thatched and had earth floors. The village pound was just beyond it on the right.*

53. *Glebe House, like most of Litton's old cottages, has been modernised but probably dates from the early 1700s.*

LITTON – The Village (2)

Apart from the church the oldest building in the village is probably Charity Farmhouse, although this was much altered in the 1700s. It may well have been the house of the Hodders as their part of the old manor was to the west of the village street. The barn, just to the west of the house, may be of the same date. On the opposite side of the road was the old Court House (the 1860 house is on the same site) with its fine old barn, often wrongly described as a tithe barn. It had six bays, a porch on the south side and a collar beamed thatched roof. The costly maintenance of the latter caused its gradual decay and the end was brought about when it was used by troops during the last war. Today only part of the walls remain. When the church could not be used during its restoration in 1877/78 the Court House Barn was licensed for worship and for marriages.

A few of the thatched cottages in Litton date from as early as the 1600s but the houses generally, especially those to the east of the church, are later. The Poor House was at the bottom of Chalk Pit Lane near its junction with Watery Lane; 19th century houses now occupy the site which was next to the village pound. The Poor Book (1795-1823) gives a good picture of the less fortunate aspects of life at the time. In particular, it shows the Barge family (the name persists in Barges Farm) falling on hard times. They had been yeomen farmers with their own small farm in the 17th century but at the beginning of the 19th John Barge, dying in the Poor House, was given a pauper's funeral and the Gladwyns were in their farm.

The Gladwyns or Gladmans have been at Litton for some three centuries as farmers and craftsmen and later as brewers and cider makers. The brewhouse, with its equipment, survives as do the nearby Malters' Cottages, still so named. It is likely that they took over the brewing business of the Hawkins family who, in the middle of the 1700s, were licensed beer retailers and had their own house under the sign of The New Inn. Perhaps they even supplied ale to the other licensed houses since in 1753 John Mowlem was landlord of The Chequers and Jasper Sergeant was at The Blue Ball. The White Horse at the bottom of the village came later; the original building was low and thatched, with a stone floor. The present inn was built when the old one was destroyed by fire in 1926.

Just below the White Horse, the Youth Hostel today occupies a building which, after the First World War, was used as a milk factory making cheese. The whey was piped down to a field further along the lane and fed to pigs; the field name is still Pig Plot.

The present building firm in Litton is the latest of a succession of family businesses. The Frys, as well as having a long history as craftsmen, have also long been associated with the church providing three consecutive generations of parsons' clerks whose duties included the daily climbing of the tower to wind the clock.

Today the upper part of the village, with its trees planted by James Cox, is designated a conservation area. The resulting strictly controlled building policy has preserved much of Litton's old-world charm.

Litton Church

Standing in a commanding position overlooking the village, St. Mary's is one of the larger churches of the valley. Of the early building only the fine 15th century tower remains unaltered. One would like to think that the nave and chancel were built by the de Gorges in the early 1300s; both, however, were to a large extent rebuilt last century.

The main restoration took place in 1877 and the faculty to carry out the work was issued in May of that year. The intention was to repair and restore the stonework of the building, remove the plaster from the walls, re-roof the nave, repair and restore the windows, take down part of the north wall and build a new transept, remove the unsafe and unsightly metal framed gallery at the back, take up and re-pave the floors and to provide entirely new seats and fittings. The old oak box pews and the fine stone three-decker pulpit were thus swept away. The cost of the whole work, which was completed in just under a year, was £820 and the re-opening took place on Easter Sunday, 1878.

During the restoration the slabs covering the Henvill graves (see under Look, page 78) beneath the nave floor were removed and their brasses detached and set into the south wall. It was at this time that the two former recesses on either side of the chancel arch were discovered as well as the piscina (drain) which would have once served a side altar. The panelled stone tablet with its painted coat of arms set in the chancel wall to the memory of George Daubney (died 1612) is considered to be a fine example of that kind of monument. The Daubneys lived at Gorwell which was then in Litton parish. An earlier burial under the chancel floor is that of William Silke who was Rector from 1434 to 1445. In his will he left Robert Randolfe, his servant, the choice of a horse, a bedstead or a cow! One would like to know which he chose.

The painting on wood of David playing the harp was originally hung on the wall of the old gallery to exhort the singers to sing, as the psalmist did, with understanding! The church effects include two small 15th century brasses long since detached from their original positions. They are unusual in that a narrow strip of brass with a latin inscription to the memory of John Chapman, fishmonger, who died in 1471 was turned over, cut in two and reused some 20 years later to commemorate John and Thomas Newpton on one piece and Alexander Warnby on the other. The older stones in the churchyard are to the Hodders, who as we have seen were an important Litton family in the 17th century and to the Sturmeys who were at Stancombe at that time.

Taylor's map (1765) shows the rectory which must have preceded the Georgian building to the west of the church. The latter was sold in 1952 and became the home of the noted engraver and typographer, Reynolds Stone, who is buried in the adjacent part of the churchyard. To replace it a new rectory, the one being used today, was built overlooking the church.

54. The oldest unaltered part of the church is the 14th century porch. The south wall of the chancel has partly restored windows of the same date but the east window is 19th century.

55. The interior of the church before the 1877 restoration described opposite.

56. *Thorner's School. The modern buildings (1968) are in front of the schoolroom built 100 years earlier. The Hollis schoolmaster's house dates from the middle of the 18th century.*

The present master of this school is a worthy old man, old-fashioned in his notions of teaching. He was assisted by his wife and by his grandson, a lad of 13. No attendance or any other record of the boys' work was kept. The schoolroom is 27 ft. by 18 ft. by 10 ft. high. Altogether there were 28 present when I visited the school. More than half of them were labourers' children, but a few were of the higher class such as policeman, tailor or blacksmith. Farmers' sons also came occasionally. They were all very young, many of them, to use their own formula, 'going in their eight or nine'. I cannot speak favourably of their attainments. There was hardly one in the upper part of the school who could read with sufficient plainness for me to understand him without following the words myself in a book. Very few attempted any sum beyond the addition of money and still fewer could divide £93 by 365. An attempt of many of the boys in the middle of the school to write out from memory the Lord's Prayer was lamentable the letters in many cases representing a conglomeration of sounds only faintly recalling the original.

Report of the Inspector for the School Enquiry Commission on Litton School from the Dorset County Chronicle, *11th February 1869.*

Thorner's School

In 1690 Robert Thorner of Baddesley, near Southampton, left property in London, the income from which was to be used towards 'the maintenance of a free school in the parish of Litton in the county of Dorsetshire, to teach the male children of the said parish to read, write, cast accounts and grammar, the schoolmaster to be nominated by the Trustees'. Robert Thorner's reason for so doing has never been established, but it is most likely that he was one of the two children of the same name baptised at Litton early in the 1700s, but a person of his standing could not have lived there without some record and there is none. A rich London merchant, coming originally from the fast-growing industrial Midlands, he was one of a group of Dissenters who, as well as promoting the Free Church, endowed a number of charities and schools as well as supporting the newly-founded University of Harvard in New England.

It is not known where Litton's first school was set up but it is probable that its master was the Thomas Davies buried in the churchyard in 1746. By about 1750 a house 'for the habitation of the schoolmaster' and a small schoolroom (18 ft. by 27 ft.) had been built by the trustees Thomas and Timothy Hollis at their own expense, this in a field called Hill Close which they had also bought. It thus became one of a number of schools, mostly in the Midlands, maintained by the group of dissenting industrialists. We know from the Hollis papers that they preferred to appoint a 'dissenting' schoolmaster but if none were available then a 'suitable churchman' was chosen. Thus at Litton the Rev. Mr. Kirkup was at the Charity School in 1793, followed by the Rev. R. Seward in 1816.

There then followed a master who 'disseminated Unitarian Principles in a manner so offensive that the parents refused to send their children to his school'. In 1834 the Charity Commissioners found that because he had refused to vacate the house, the Trustees had spent no money on the repairs of the buildings. Their recommendation that the schoolroom should be rebuilt was not followed until 40 years later. Ten years after an adverse report by the School Enquiry Commission in 1868 the villlage took matters into its own hands and raised, by public subscription, the £230 necessary to provide the schoolroom which still serves as part of the present school.

From then on, although the Thorner's Trust was still the legal owner and the now small payment from the Charity was still made, the school was managed by six governors, four appointed by the Trustees and two by the Subscribers' Committee. The education side was at that time taken over by the Board of Education and later by the Local Authority but the village had to maintain the buildings. After a few years as a small central school for older children, it became the junior and infant school which it remains today. In 1950 the managers, faced with the impossible task of bringing the buildings up to standard, persuaded the Diocesan Education Committee that it was a church school and so it became, with its fine new building, Thorner's Voluntary Aided Church of England School – not exactly in line with the founder's intent or with his inclination in church matters!

Higher and Lower Coombe

Hutchins has no early history of Coombe which he refers to separately as Coomb Temple and Comb Abbas; he also suggests that the former was so called as it once belonged to the Knights Templar and that the latter once belonged to a religious house. It seems, however, that there is no historical evidence for this.

It is clear from later mediæval records that 'Cumb' was an individual manor in Litton parish and held in the same way by the de Gorges as part of the greater manor of Chewton in Somerset. Thomas, the parson of Puncknowle, who poached Ralph de Gorges' fish at Litton, was also summoned for taking goods to the value of 100 s. at Cumb in the following year (1268). In 1316 John de Gorges had, 'in Cumbe juxta (next to) Ludeton, 1 messuage (dwelling house), 2 chambers, 1 chapel, 1 cowshed, 1 carthorse, 50 acres of wood, 100 apple trees and 200 osiers'. By the end of the 14th century, Coombe, as with Litton, was in the ownership of the Cheneys and Russells – in 1386 Ralph Cheyne and Maurice Russell held jointly 1 messuage and 3 carucates of land there.

Its subsequent story is very much the same as that of Litton's manor farm. By Elizabeth's time it belonged to the Hurdings and continued with them until 1703 when it became part of the Richards' estate. From them it was bought by the Longs of Salisbury and since then has changed hands a number of times. Generally its tenants seem to have related more closely to nearby Chilcombe though for parish purposes it belonged to Litton.

Stancombe

Though in Litton parish, this farm is right on the boundary with Askerswell and geographically in the valley at the head of the Asker River. The earliest record found is in 1490 which refers to 'a tenant and ferling of land in Fursyn in the manor of Stancombe and a quarry of tiling stone there'. The name, of course, means the 'valley with stones'. The Sturmeys who lived there had headstones in Litton churchyard which are among the earliest noted for that parish.

North Eggardon Farm

This is indeed remote from the Bride Valley but was, until 1889, a parcel of the parish of Litton reaching as far north as Eggardon Hill Fort and southward to the Asker. The parish boundary ran (and still does) through the middle of the hill fort so that the southern half of the earthwork was in Litton parish. It has often been confused historically with Loders Matravers to the west and South Eggardon Farm to the east. In the 13th and 14th centuries it was the Lodres Lutton which at least one place name authority has confused with Matravers and Lodres Bingham. To the people of Litton in the 1700s it was familiarly known as Loderland and regarded parochially as something of a nuisance. As a manor it had always been held by lords who had no lands in the Bride Valley and how it came to be part of Litton parish is a mystery yet to be solved.

57. *Storm over Higher Coombe. Askers Roadhouse on the skyline. The Iron Age settlement was on the spur to the left.*

58. *Stancome, north of the A35, is part of Litton parish at the head of the Asker Valley*

59. *Chilcombe. The farmhouse (centre) dwarfs the church which is just left of the group of buildings. A telephoto view from Hodders Hill three-quarters of a mile to the east.*

60. *The stone which was over the north door of the now vanished mansion of the Bishops.*

CHILCOMBE

One of the smallest parishes in the county, the Chilcombe of today represents the Saxon manor recorded in the Domesday Survey held by Brictuin, one of the king's thegns. As such he was one of the Saxon landowners who were allowed to retain their manors after the Norman Conquest. In 'Ciltecumb' there was land for three ploughs, two of them, in the demesne farm; one villein and eights bordars had 'half a plough' between them. A mill was also recorded which must have been down on the Bride which then, as today, formed the southern boundary of the parish. The name means 'cold valley' and this led Hutchins to suggest that the ancient village was in the valley bottom east of the church on the hill but there is no archaeological evidence for this.

From the later Middle Ages to Tudor times Chilcombe was held by The Knights Hospitallers of St. John of Jerusalem, their early tenants being a family which took its name from the manor – de Childecombe. During the reign of Henry VIII it was granted to William Bishop whose family were to hold it for seven generations. Part of Chilcombe's lands they let for a while to the Martins of Longbredy – William's grandson in fact married a Martin. His father was the John who built, or perhaps more likely rebuilt the old manor house which stood west of the little church. Hutchins described it as a low, pretty large, plain and ancient building of stone built round a quadrangle. Over the door was a stone inscribed 'Anno Dmi 1578 John Byssop Elnor Byssop'. The 'Elnor' was John's wife Eleanor. The building survived until 1939 although by that time it was in a state of decay and had to be demolished.

The last of the Bishops, Humphry, died in 1709 and the manor of Chilcombe passed to John Foyle, a Wiltshire landowner, who had married his sister. The farm and lands were now let to Francis and Mary Roberts who came to Chilcombe from Wales and whose descendants were, as we shall see later, to play an important part in the life of the valley. They were followed by the Strongs whose memorials are prominent in the church and who farmed there for the next 100 years. The present house must have been built in their time, during the latter part of the 18th century, as was the stone barn which was put up in 1816. After the Strongs, came their cousins the Samways family who had farmed at Loders. They rented, and later bought, the 300 acres which made up the Chilcombe farm, from the Nelson family to whom it had passed by marriage. The Samways were noted for their flock of Dorset Horn sheep during their occupation of Chilcombe which lasted until early this century.

Here, as elsewhere in the valley, the 20th century has brought about the disintegration of a clearly defined unit of land which has been under one ownership for over 1000 years. While the parish boundaries remain for administrative purposes they no longer define lands held by different individuals. Thus at Chilcombe the house is divorced from the farm and the land is shared by farms in the adjacent parishes.

CHILCOMBE

The parish boundary on the north side is only 700 yards long, its position probably determined by the 23-acre hill-fort, 650 feet above sea level, which crowns the hill overlooking the church. The heart-shaped enclosure has a single rampart and such enclosures are usually considered to be of late Bronze or early Iron Age date. There are no traces of occupation within and, since its defences are very slight, it may well have been an animal compound rather than a fort (Fig. 3, 15).

Below it one wonders how the tiny parish of Chilcombe has managed to survive. Its mediæval neighbour Sturthill succumbed to the depopulation and change of land usage that followed the Black Death in the middle of the 1300s. Chilcombe too had its lean times; a church record of 1425 noted that at that time, and for a long time before, no services had been held 'propter exilitatem' – the literal meeting of the Latin 'on account of thinness' may have been intended to imply poverty on a wide scale.

A 'Muster Roll' of men able to carry arms, taken in 1542 listed six in Chilcombe, five Jessops and one Bryant. By then the mediæval village had dwindled to what was virtually a family farm and this is borne out by the Hearth of Tax of 1662. This tax, an ingenious way of making up a huge deficiency in the Government's revenue, generally meant counting chimneys – at Chilcombe there were 14, nine of them on Henry Bishop's manor house leaving but five for the cottages. Chilcombe must then have been very much as it is today, a fact which makes the survival of the church all the more remarkable.

The mediæval village was approached, as today, by a road up from the valley which continued northwards to the high road. There was, however, another which ran from Shipton, through Sturthill and up the hill to Chilcombe just south of the village. Crossing the other road, it then ran down the hill to Lower Coombe and then on to Litton. This old route is today a bridleway and in many places along it the hollows of the old road can still be seen. Surface features in the field west of the two cottages suggest that the old village, never very large, extended from the church along the south-east slope of the hill to the crossroad thus formed.

The 18th century farmhouse is now the home of the American artist, John Hubbard, who happily has the same care for the nearby little church as did those in the manor house for centuries before him. The rest of the village of Chilcombe is made up of two 19th century cottages not far from the old crossroads.

Hutchins writes of a salt spring 'much frequented by pigeons'. Today this shows as a tiny patch of grass, somewhat brackish-looking, in a cultivated field between Rudge and the river. Traditionally regarded to have healing power, there was a suggestion last century, when 'spas' were in vogue, that it should be commercially exploited but this came to nothing because of a dispute as to mineral rights! Analysis of the water carried out for the writer shows it to have a salinity about 10 per cent that of sea water.

61. *Chilcombe House today is the modernised 18th century farmhouse which was built along the south of the quadrangle of the Elizabethan house.*

62. *Chilcombe had a tradition of being involved in smuggling. This tunnel, discovered in 1890 was reputed to have been an illicit store. It is blocked off some 10 foot from the mouth and is more likely to have been the entrance to an ice-well.*

63. *The church has no known dedication. Both the building and the furnishings seem like diminutive versions of the typical parish church.*

64. *The off-set chancel arch makes room for the memorial to John Bishop who died in 1682. The chair given by his great uncle Richard Bishop is behind the lectern.*

CHILCOMBE – The Church

The building is tiny and in keeping with the parish, so that a congregation of 40 would fill it to capacity. In size and form it has probably little changed over 1000 years. The basic masonry is Norman but there was a partial rebuilding in the early 15th century. It was restored about a 100 years ago without drastically altering the ancient fabric. The 12th century chancel is about 11 ft. square, the size of a small living room; the nave (21 ft. by 15 ft.) has been much rebuilt but the south wall and doorway were built in Norman times. Unusually the chancel is offset so that its north wall and that of the nave are in a straight line.

The fittings range from a Norman font to a 19th century carved stone altar. An armchair carved with RB 1642, a wall tablet in memory of John Bishop, 1682, and as part of the church plate a chalice inscribed with the date 1673 and the arms of the Bishops remind us of that family's long stay at Chilcombe. The wooden panel in the chancel, with its three pokerwork scenes, was traditionally supposed to have come from the wreck of a ship of the Spanish Armada. The Royal Commission and others have considered it to have been a reredos (a screen made to go on the wall behind the altar) but one expert considers it to have been the front of a chest. All agree that it is some 100 years later than the Armada and certainly foreign in origin.

Memorials to the Strongs figure prominently in the church and churchyard, the latter so small that it must be only a part of the original graveyard. In fact Hutchins noted that there was, between the church and the old mansion, 'A small enclosure, well-fenced, where human bones have at times been dug'. More have been found since then and this was, no doubt, the site of the mediæval burying place.

From the earliest record in 1310 to the breaking up of the monasteries, except when the de Childcombs held the living in the 14th century, the successive Priors of the Knights Templar presented the parsons; there was constant change, perhaps because of the poverty of the parish. It is worth noting that Chilcombe lost its rector in the Black Death – five other parishes in the valley suffered in the same way. Appointments continued to be made by the Bishops and later owners of the manor until the last century when Chilcombe was linked with one or other of its neighbouring churches, but never, it seems, for very long at a time. In 1954 it was united with Burton Bradstock and is now one of the Bride Valley Group.

There are no early registers for the parish, the present ones beginning in 1813. By Hutchins' time the little acreage of glebeland which was allocated to the parson was already lost and he was allowed £29 a year out of the farm. One cannot help coming to the conclusion that the little church has, for most of its existence, been virtually a private chapel for the residents of the manor house; it is indeed likely that, even at its highest, the population of the parish could always be accommodated.

PUNCKNOWLE – Romano-British Sites

After the excavation at Pins Knoll on the north side of the valley, attention was turned to a field on the south side just over a quarter of a mile to the east of Puncknowle Knoll, its name 'Walls' suggesting the possibility of buried building remains. Systematic search for several years, particularly during cultivation, indicated an extensive Romano-British settlement and this was confirmed by a trial excavation in 1964 which showed, however, that the site was virtually ploughed out (Fig. 3, 10).

The following year the search was carried into the adjoining field on the south side where the ground level was higher and where, it was hoped, there had been less destruction. This proved to be the case and thus began what was to become four seasons' work which revealed a complex system of stone walling, the exact nature of which is still uncertain. The air photograph shows a walled enclosure, 90 ft. long and 60 ft. wide, rectangular in shape save for the eastern side which was curved. Within the latter was a small building with a floor of pitched stones, the rest of the enclosed area being paved and cobbled to form a kind of courtyard which was kept free of rain water by a system of stone-lined drains. An outer wall, running parallel to the central enclosure, made a corridor which was almost certainly roofed.

Surface indications in the two fields, together with observation of drainage trenches which were dug in Walls, showed the stone complex to be the centre of an area of occupation about 150 yards across, cut through by the mediæval parish boundary between Puncknowle and Bexington. The boundary ran diagonally across the enclosure, of which the half on the Walls side had been ploughed out leaving no trace.

The pottery and coin evidence from the excavation showed that people were living on the site from before the Roman Invasion and continued throughout the Occupation, especially during the last 200 years. We can be certain that the enclosure complex was in use between AD350 and 390. Its purpose must be conjectural but nothing was found during the subsequent excavation to contradict the early conclusion that here was a Roman-Celtic temple. The area around such shrines was generally regarded as sacred ground and enclosed by a boundary wall within which was the 'cella' which housed the cult images and could only be entered by the priest. If in our case the cella was the small building at the east end of the enclosure then the courtyard formed a large area for activities associated with the shrine. Certainly the cobbling of the latter was well worn and hundreds of nails from footware were found on it. The absence of hearths and domestic debris within the enclosure also pointed to a use other than domestic.

The vast quantity of stone necessary came from quarries not more than 200 yards to the south. What remained must have been only a small part of the original and it was possible to show that the Romano-British site itself had been used as a quarry in the Middle Ages.

Two crouched burials were found beneath the enclosure and a third was found some distance away during drainage work on Walls. The latter was accompanied by a bowl which showed its owner to have lived just before, or perhaps a little after, the Roman Invasion of AD43.

65. *The view from The Knoll south of Puncknowle village. It looks east across the Romano-British settlement site to the Iron Age hill-fort on the skyline.*

66. *The 'Walls' excavation (1968) looking south. Later work showed that the enclosure extended to the field wall along the bottom of the photograph but beyond it had been destroyed by ploughing.*

67, 68.   The burial on the east side of The Knoll poses many questions; in particular whether it was associated with the settlement in Walls.

mm

69.   A cornelian ring-stone found on the settlement site dates from Roman Britain. The cut-out figure is that of a sea centaur – half human, half horse.

Photo: E. Flatters.

PUNCKNOWLE – Romano-British Sites on The Knoll

If the site in Walls was that of a temple it must have been a meeting place for those living in the 10 other settlements in the valley and, of course, there were no doubt others long since obliterated.

The Iron Age folk tended to bury their dead within their occupation area in any convenient spot. This continued into the Roman Occupation but gave way under Roman influence, to cemeteries away from habitation. In the same way the crouched burial in an oval grave gave way to extended graves, side by side, in orderly fashion. A possible clue to the position of the cemetery associated with the later phase of the Walls site came when the plough struck what seemed to be a buried wall in the small field on the east side of the Knoll (Fig. 3, 11). Investigation revealed not a wall but four blocks of limestone laid in line, each block about 20 ins. square and 9 ins. thick. They were set at right angles to the contour of the hill and appeared to mark a grave with an east-west orientation. Subsequent excavation exposed an extended male skeleton. No coffin nails were found but the 'shadow' of a coffin showed plainly in the light coloured soil and the front of the skull had been crushed, apparently by the collapse of the coffin lid. Late Romano-British pottery sherds were found at all levels in the fill of the grave but the body had no grave goods.

Such a sophisticated burial must have been that of an individual of some high social standing. The stones, dressed by an expert mason, must have come either from Portland or, more likely, from the quarry above Portesham. Such a grave, with its east-west alignment, would be consistent with late Romano-British custom but the stones are unusual. It is difficult to believe that this is an isolated burial but only excavation could show if there are others.

Field work has shown that in the vicinity of the grave on the east side of the Knoll, and again on the north between the hill and the village, there were other Romano-British settlements (Fig. 3, 10), perhaps in some way associated with the Walls site. The pottery found there included red 'Samian' ware, a Roman fabric which is easily identified and readily dated to the earlier years of the Roman Occupation. Here too was found the lower stone of a rotary quern of the type used by Iron Age people to grind corn, suggesting that the period of occupation of the Knoll site was very much in line with that at Walls.

The chalk of the southern hills which lie between the upper Bride Valley and the sea gives way, west of Abbotsbury hill-fort, to limestones and clays. Puncknowle Knoll is an isolated greensand cap once part of the great sheet laid down at the bottom of the chalk-forming sea. During the search for sites in the valley it came as something of a surprise that there should have been pre-Roman settlements on the not so easily cultivated clays. Here, as elsewhere in the valley, an Iron Age/Romano-British site has been followed by an Anglo-Saxon village close by.

PUNCKNOWLE – The Manor

Various explanations of the first element of the name have been put forward without any certainty; the second, of course, refers to the round-topped hill to the south of the village, which, rising prominently to almost 600 ft. above sea level, is still called The Knoll.

The mediæval parish was small; only Chilcombe of the Bride Valley parishes was smaller. Its size was doubled in the 15th century by the addition of Bexington. The spelling of the name with its pronunciation 'Punnle' has always caused difficulty. The nearest the Domesday Book scribe could get 900 years ago was 'Pomecanole'. Then it was taxed for five hides and had land for four ploughs with a total value of £5. This may be compared with Bexington's nine and a half hides, seven ploughs and a value of £6. The constant change of owner in the later Middle Ages reflects the low value of the parish as a source of income. It is not by chance that most of the valley's villages are north of the river on the south facing slope with its lighter soils. Hutchins lists eight families from the Whytefields in the late 1200s to the Duke of Clarence 200 years later. None of them seems to have lived at Puncknowle and little is known of their tenants. Not until the Napiers came to settle in the valley does the record become more certain.

This family, with its alternative name Napper, came, according to their monument in Swyre Church 'out of Scotland' at the end of the 15th century. Their story in the valley begins early in the 1500s when James Napier, who already had relations elsewhere in Dorset, came to Puncknowle. His son, another James, married Anne Russell of Berwick and from their descendants emerged two more lines of Napiers who, in the next 100 years had acquired the manors and built themselves new houses at Puncknowle, Bexington and Baglake. It seems that James lived at Swyre but the site of the manor is not known. The Napier interest in the area lasted until early in the 18th century when they forsook Puncknowle Manor for their already established seat at Moor Crichel in East Dorset.

The estate was sold to William Clutterbuck, described by Hutchins as 'a sea officer who came out of Devon'. William had married into the Chafin family of Chettle House in North Dorset and during the 100 years or so of the association of the Clutterbucks with Puncknowle they were closely linked with that part of the county. John, William's son, appointed the former Rector of Farnham to Puncknowle and after him the Rector of Tollard Royal who had married his sister. Their son George followed his father as Rector of Puncknowle but in 1804 moved to Litton Rectory so that his nephew, the Rev. George Clutterbuck Frome, could take over Puncknowle. It was through the marriage of the latter that the manor of Puncknowle came to the Mansels who lived there during the latter half of the last century.

Not all the land in Puncknowle belonged to the manor as there were several freehold properties which belonged to the Sheridans. The greater part of the old manor of Puncknowle, however, still remains intact as part of the Bridgeman Estates.

70. *The east front and porch which the Napiers added to their 16th century manor house around 1650. The west wing has been replaced with a modern building.*

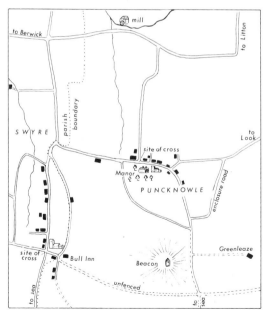

71. *Puncknowle and Swyre in the 1700s.*

72. The centre of the village with remains of the stocks in front of the lych-gate of the church.

73. The little house on The Knoll is prominent both as a landmark and a sea-mark.

PUNCKNOWLE – The Village

The small Norman church, with its adjacent manor house, is in an attractive setting and forms the nucleus of the village. The parish, now with Bexington added, extends from the sea to the Bride. We have already noticed how the boundary gave access to the river to enable the parish to have its mill. The first is mentioned in 1086, when it was valued at 12s. 6d. – higher than any other mill in the valley. The last, probably on or near the same site, continued to work until well into this century. It has now been converted into a private house.

The centre of Puncknowle, with its much weathered stone houses, has an old-world charm, though only the manor is earlier than the 18th century. It seems likely that its east block was added in Jacobean times to the house which the Napiers had built a century before. The older building was demolished last century and replaced with the present west wing. The attractive east front has its wide central porch flanked by arched mullioned windows which, in turn, reflect the curved arch of the doorway. Inside, the house still retains many original features.

Throughout its early history, the manor was let to tenants who, no doubt, found the farm difficult to manage. The 19th century field pattern suggests that there were originally three open fields, though there is no documentary evidence for this. The East Field was on that side of Clay Lane north of the Bexington boundary, the West Field between The Knoll and Bull Lane which marked the boundary with Swyre and the North Field between Hazel Lane and the road to Litton. The East Field still has 'The Drives' which was a wide strip of common land, left after the enclosure of the open field, enabling animals to be driven to and from the new 'closes'.

The 15th century cross, with its octagonal shaft and moulded capping, is now in the churchyard but once, according to tradition, stood at the junction of Rectory Lane with the High Street. The wide road was probably the site of the village green, where, near the church lych-gate, the lower stone part of the village stocks still remain. The school, now the Village Hall, dates from the middle of the last century but there must have been an earlier one of sorts – in 1668 Gregory Winter was licensed, by the Bishop of Bristol, 'to teach a school at Puncknowll'.

The reason for the little house with one room up and one down, which stands on the Knoll, has been the cause of much speculation. It is, in fact, built on a Bronze Age barrow and a cremation urn, now in the County Museum, was found beneath the house foundations early this century. With its commanding view over the whole of Lyme Bay, it has been suggested that it was a coastguard look-out. On the other hand, we know that the Knoll was the site of a signal station, one of a chain strung along the south coast in 1794, and the house could well have been associated with it. The Royal Commission, whose task it was to record all buildings up to 1714, and later if they thought fit, chose to ignore it, though the fireplace suggests a late 18th century date. Certainly, Taylor (1765) shows 'Puncknoll Beacon' on the Knoll.

PUNCKNOWLE – The Church of St. Mary

The small church is best considered without the recent (1891) addition of the north aisle. The impression within is one of age but of the Norman building only the tower and chancel arch retain any of the original fabric. The 12th century tower arch was heightened and rebuilt in 1678 at the expense of Robert Napier and his wife whose initials, with the date, are on the keystone of the arch. The tower doorway was built at the same time and still has its original door and lock and the initials R N picked out in nail studs.

The tiny south aisle, built or perhaps rebuilt in 1660, was according to tradition originally for the use of the Bexington folk who had lost their church. The reasons for this are discussed later. One strongly suspects, however, that the Napiers, who were obviously much concerned with the church, soon came to regard the south aisle as their own private chapel and were buried in the vault beneath it. Almost all the family which descended from James of Swyre seem to have found a last resting place at Puncknowle and it is clear that they regarded Puncknowle Church as 'their' church. The father of the last of the Puncknowle Napiers was the Sir Robert whose memorial is on the south wall of the nave. It was he who had erected the memorial to his father (the Robert who was responsible for much of the 17th century restoration of the church). Before the north aisle was built it was on the north wall of the nave.

The defaced and whitewashed remains of a wall painting above the chancel arch has three panels with borders of red roses and black lines but the central motifs are lost. The Royal Commission considered it to be most likely of Tudor origin. It has recently been shown that it overlies an earlier, perhaps mediæval, mural.

Hutchins gives a list of the parsons at Puncknowle from 1321 onwards. Three more can be added, John Stule in 1305, Thomas Belgrave in 1384 and the notorious Thomas who, as we have seen (under Litton) poached Ralph de Gorges deer in 1267. He seems also to have been a common thief who, with others, was taken to the same court by Nicholas de la Toure who complained that they had taken goods from his house at Swyre.

In 1642, when John Croft was Rector, 49 males over the age of 18 and then living in Puncknowle parish signed the Protestation binding themselves to uphold and defend the true Protestant Religion. The Longbredy return recorded that John Napper of Baglake, a Popish recusant (one who refused to attend Church of England services) and William and Edward Warham (his brothers-in-law) were 'not to be spoken to by us'. John Napper died in 1644 and in his will desired to be buried in the church of Puncknowle 'where lyeth my wife Elizabeth'. But, he added, 'tymes are such as whether Anabaptist . . . and such heretics will give it (meaning his body) Christian Buriall noe man knows'. Being afraid that his worst fears might be realised and burial at Puncknowle refused, he gave directions that if that were the case he was to be buried in his garden at Baglake. Let us hope he was accepted at Puncknowle – unfortunately, the register of burials from 1642 to 1660 is missing and we shall never know.

74. *Church and manor house form the nucleus of the village as they have done since mediæval times.*

75. *Movement of the mediæval cross from its traditional site in the village must have taken place before 1770 as Hutchins recorded it in its present position.*

76, 77.   Richard Henville's house 'Lower Look' was built, as is shown on the lintel of the south door, in 1700.

78.   The date-stone of the demolished 'Higher Look' has been built into a wall at the rear of the farmhouse.

Look Farm in Puncknowle

This narrow wedge-shaped manor extended southwards from its broad end, which ran along the Bride, to a point just north of Abbotsbury Hill-fort. Today it is in Puncknowle parish but in Hutchins' time was part of Abbotsbury. He mistakenly thought it was the 'Lahoc' of the Domesday Book which was in fact Hooke near Beaminster. His account of Look begins in 1539 at the dissolution of Abbotsbury Abbey; at that time it was part of the monastic lands. However, earlier records show that it has been in the possession of other monastic foundations, both of them Cistercian. Thus in 1234 a charter mentions the 'land of Nottington and Luca, purchased by Gilbert de Percy from the monks of Forde and bestowed on Bindon'. Records further suggest that from Bindon it passed to the Benedictines of Abbotsbury before 1337.

At the Dissolution, Look was bought by the Tregonwells who had also acquired Milton Abbas; they let it in 1629 to Ralph Henvill for the lives of his three sons. It seems that between them the mediæval manor was divided into two forms; the existing house, perhaps rebuilt by the Henvills in 1652 became Higher Look and the home of successive generations all bearing the name Edward. Close by, about 300 yards of less down the little stream, Richard Henvill, Ralph's grandson, built his somewhat unorthodox house at Lower Look which stills stands. The Henvills themselves were of some standing in the county of Dorset; in fact Richard was High Sheriff in 1723. They had, of course, by this time purchased the manor from the Tregonwells. Contemporary with the Hodders of Litton and the Hurdings of Longbredy they regarded Litton as their church and several of them lie buried under its nave floor.

The last Edward Henvill sold Higher Look in 1770, Lower Look having already been sold by Richard. From then on the former seems to have ceased to be a separate farm and the house was converted into cottages. Lower Look then became the farmhouse of the two farms which had been united under one owner, the Brownes of Frampton, and later the Sheridans. The estate was sold off by them this century and today Ralph Henvill's house is the nucleus of a family farm. It was said that at one time there were nine cottages at Look; traces of some of them can still be found but only one is still standing.

It is likely that the Abbotsbury Abbey's Look Farm was on or near the site of that today. An old road can be traced connecting the two places via Ashley and Gorwell Gate. It has also been pointed out that Look, with its older name, forms 'Luk' in 1212 and 'Luca' in 1234 less than a mile from the Chapel of St. Luke in Ashley. A connection between the two has been suggested but (as has been shown on page 42) the two not only belonged to two separate manors but were also held by two different monasteries, the one Cistercian, the other Benedictine. No documentary reference has been found so far confirming the dedication of the chapel, but Hutchins, though he could find nothing of its history, confidently asserted 'here was a chapel dedicated to St. Luke'.

BEXINGTON

The ancient parish lay between Puncknowle and the sea and in 1086 was held by Roger de Arundel, a Norman knight. It was taxed for nine and three-quarter hides and had land for seven ploughs, its value was somewhat greater than that of its neighbour. Roger's granddaughter Maud gave Bexington to the newly founded Abbey of Bindon but the right to present the parson she gave, together with some land, to nearby Abbotsbury. At the dissolution of the monasteries the manor was bought by John Caryl and was sold to the Napiers towards the end of the reign of Elizabeth.

By this time the mediæval village as such had ceased to exist. The story of the sacking of Bexington by French pirates in 1440 is well known but all the evidence points to the fact that the village was, by then, already in a state of decay. In 1451 the Bishop declared Bexington to be 'united' with Puncknowle and ordered the Rector of St. Mary's to celebrate Mass once a week and on the day of the Patronal Festival in the chancel of St. Giles at Bexington. He was further instructed to repair the chancel, presumably after the ravages of the pirates; in return he was granted the tithes of Bexington. It is likely that the repair was never carried out; instead a small aisle was built on to Puncknowle Church for the use of the few remaining people of Bexington. The church of St. Giles was vaguely described by Hutchins as 'near the sea' but it is probable that it was close to the Manor House, where human remains disturbed by earth-moving during the war and skeletons recorded by the writer in builders' trenches in the 1950s, suggest the site of the mediæval graveyard.

The forerunner of the present 'Manor House' was built by the Napiers and all the indications are that at the time there were few, if any, cottages of the old village remaining. Taylor's map, drawn up about the same time as the Napiers sold Bexington (as they did Puncknowle) to the Clutterbucks, shows a farmhouse and no cottages. This is corroborated by the first Ordnance Survey map published in 1811 which showed buildings associated with the farmhouse but no other cottages. Bexington thus continued as an isolated farm with a row of labourer's cottages (now Tamarisk Farm) added. In the latter part of the last century it was let to the Palmers who eventually bought Puncknowle Manor. The old land unit continued until it was broken up in the 1920s and an abortive attempt was made to establish 'Bexington-on-Sea' as a potential seaside resort. One wonders what would have happened to Bexington if, as was seriously considered in the 1890s, the railway to Abbotsbury had been continued along the coast to Bridport and beyond.

East Bexington is now in Abbotsbury parish. It is likely that it was the parcel of land which Maud de Arundel gave to the Abbey in the 12th century so that at the dissolution it passed, as did Abbotsbury itself, to Sir Giles Strangeways. It remained in Bexington parish until 1889 when it was transferred to Abbotsbury to compensate their losing Look to Puncknowle. The boundary used to run from the hill-fort to the sea; it now runs from Tulks Hill about 600 yards to the west of the original line.

79. *The likely site of the church of St. Giles. The mill and barn on the left and the 'Manor House' on the right are the successors to the Napier's farm buildings.*

80. *The font of Puncknowle Church is made up of two bowls, one upon the other. Both are late 12th century. It is quite possible that the lower came from St. Giles.*

81. *Swyre village from the south-west. The manor farm complex on the right was rebuilt by the Bedford Estate early last century.*

82. *The stone walls which make up the field boundaries remind us that this is a limestone area.*

SWYRE – The Manor

The parish now, as in mediæval times, extends from the Bride to the sea. The name comes from an Old English word meaning a neck of land joining two hills, aptly describing the position of the village. In the Domesday Book Swyre is entered as belonging to William de Eu, an important Norman baron. It was large, with the value of £9 put on nine hides with land for seven ploughs.

In the 13th century the manor was held by the de la Lynde family as part of the lands of Henry de Novo Burgo who lived at, and added his name to Winfrith (Newburgh) elsewhere in the county. Walter de la Lynde, who was at Swyre in 1270, then claimed the wreck of the sea, free chase and warren with the right to a gallows. A court case relates how the latter was 'knocked down' by a number of locals. The manor then passed to William de Monte Acuto; his son Simon had occasion to complain that Edward de Bonvil (he lived at what is now Bredy further down the valley) with others, 'took 2 chests of coined money and other goods value 300 marks thrown on the land within the manor of Swyre'. Simon, like his predecessors, jealously claimed his right to anything washed up on the beach. After the Montacutes, who left Swyre in the early 1400s, the manor was controlled by the Crown.

The Napiers seem to have first settled there during the latter part of the reign of Henry VII because it was then that James Napier 'of Swyre' married Anne Russell, daughter of John Russell of Berwick. Anne, as we shall see later, was the sister of James Russell whose son John became the 1st Earl of Bedford. The Napiers, however, had left Swyre by 1584 and it passed to the Harbins of North Dorset who in turn sold it to the then Duke of Bedford in 1660. This was part of the policy of the later Bedfords who gradually bought those manors in the valley which they considered to be part of their family heritage.

The parish of Swyre did not consist of that manor alone. Berwick was part of it and, as we shall see later, was generally in different hands. Between Berwick and the Burton boundary lay the small manor of Modbury. Traces of it can still be seen on either side where the Burton road passes over a distinct hump west of Berwick. Hutchins, in 1760, described it as 'a hamlet where ruins and foundation appear on both sides of the road, depopulated beyond the memory of man'. The name, Modberghe in old forms, originally signified a mound used as a meeting place. In early records it is often described as 'next to Sturtel'.

The site of Chaldecote (the cold cottage), which occurs frequently in early records relating to Swyre parish, has been lost. One has a strong suspicion that it was where Clayhanger is today, in the little valley leading down from Swyre to Berwick.

Although the Ordnance Survey map shows 'Swyre Barrow' on the coast road, the denuded mound has not been considered as prehistoric. It may have been a beacon site; the possibility of this is discussed below. Between it and Berwick House, in a field called Oxclose, the site of a Romano-British settlement was found after the plough had turned up worked stone (Fig. 3, 12) and subsequent trial excavation provided evidence of occupation. It had, however, been virtually destroyed by cultivation.

SWYRE – The Village

Although some three-quarters of a mile from the beach, Swyre has always been associated with the sea – in fact, it was said of the inhabitants late in the 18th century, that they were 'of the hybrid character of fisherman, smugglers and labourers, their energies mainly devoted to the two former occupations'. They had their direct communication with the beach by the lane which then ran on as a continuation of the present road through the village.

No doubt the mediæval house pattern was very much the same as today, the tofts or homesteads strung along the main street with their small plots running down into the little valley and up the other side to Back Lane. Hutchins says that the common fields were enclosed in 1666, but it has not been possible to work out where they were, in spite of the fact that, of all the parishes in the valley, Swyre has the most regular pattern of field enclosure which suggests that the open system was brought to an end fairly quickly.

The village as we see it today is little changed from that of the middle of the last century when the Duke of Bedford carried out a rehousing programme. His agent had allowed the estate at Swyre to run down; it was let as a small main farm and a number of smaller holdings, neither of which was a profitable concern and the general picture of the village in the early 1800s was one of abject poverty. An effort was made to improve the social conditions of the Swyre folk and, as we shall see later, to do something about what was described as their declining morals. Swyre farmhouse was rebuilt and gradually the old cottages along the street were replaced with the small, stone, grey-coloured houses which are still there with their dates of construction; the date of a Bedford house can invariably be found below a crown and 'B' on a plaque high up on the gable end. The houses at Swyre were built 'with every convenience for health, cleanliness and comfort, after the designs of the Duke himself'.

Fishing (with its sideline smuggling) was, as we have seen, a major occupation. There was once on Swyre beach, at the bottom of the lane from the village, a little stone house called 'The White House', rebuilt by William Russell, Earl of Bedford, in 1667, as a shelter for fishermen and shipwrecked mariners; its site was marked on the earlier Ordnance Survey maps. The Protestation return for Swyre (1642) is relevant – 50 males over the age of 18 signed but some were recorded as unable to do so 'being gone away toward the sea in voyages, some for Newfoundland'. No doubt they sailed from Bridport which had, because of its net and tackle industry, become associated with the Newfoundland fishery.

The limestone quarries south of the coast road, just south-west of the village, were once extensively worked for building stone as well as for lime-burning for 'manure' which was used on the clay slopes which face the sea. To the west of the village is the hill 'Beacon Knap'. No documentary evidence has been found to support there being a station there and it surely was too close to Puncknowle Knoll with its confirmed site. The name, however, still persists in Swyre, the field at the top of the hill being 'Becken' – the 'Beacon' of the 1836 Tithe Map.

83.   *The Bedford houses were sold off when the Swyre estate was broken up. Although modernised their basic form is unaltered.*

84.   *Swyre Cross. The base of a mediæval cross can be seen between the war memorial and the signpost. The Bull Inn (behind the tree on the left) is in Puncknowle parish.*

85. *Berwick House. All that remains of the building described by Hutchins is the wing facing the road. The original house was built round a quadrangle with the principle entrance on the west side.*

86. *A view of Berwick from the south in the early 1800s, painted by John Baverstock Knight. The large barn remains but has been re-roofed.*

Berwick

Berwick's claim to fame lies in the fact that it was the birth-place of the John Russell who was to become the 1st Duke of Bedford and the founder of a family which, from Tudor times, has been prominent in national affairs. The story of John's transition from farmer's son to courtier has often been told and no doubt embellished in the telling. In January, 1506, a ship carrying the daughter of the King and Queen of Castile and her husband Philip, Archduke of Austria, had been forced to put in to Weymouth by bad weather. The royal couple were entertained by Sir John Trenchard at Wolfeton House near Dorchester and John Russell, because he could speak Spanish, was called upon to act as interpreter. He accompanied the party to the Court at Windsor where he caught the attention of the King and, becoming established as a courtier, rose during the next 30 years to positions of high standing.

John was the son of the James Russell whose brass is in Swyre Church. Little is known of the father except that he farmed some of the Berwick lands and lived in Little Berwick near the Manor House which was the home of the older John Russell who was probably his father.

The pedigree of the Russells of Berwick has been the subject of much research with varying conclusions. As we have seen, an older branch of the Russell family had lived (and died out) further up the valley at Kingston Russell; much effort was made by earlier genealogists to establish a link between the two families and it is certain that the early Dukes of Bedford believed themselves to be descended from both families and that is why they bought Kingston Russell when the opportunity arose.

Modern research has failed to show how they might be connected and John's earliest traceable ancestor appears to have been Stephen Russell, a well-to-do Weymouth merchant with a fleet of ships trading with foreign parts. He was several times Member of Parliament for the Borough early in the 1400s. Anciently the Berwick Manor had been held by the de la Tours and Stephen's association with the Bride Valley came with his marrying the heiress to the manor. Alice (her other name is not known) proved her claim in 1422 at a court in Dorchester, it being established that she was descended from the de la Tours. Her grandson John may have been the first Russell at Berwick.

While the younger John was rising to fame, the rest of the Berwick family faded into obscurity. In the time of Elizabeth the manor was leased by the Greys of Askerwell; they were followed in the 1600s and early 1700s by the Squibbs and their relations the Gollops; both the latter buried at Swyre. When the lease ran out the Bedford Estate rebuilt the house making it much smaller. The old building, which Hutchins must have known well, was described by him as an ancient and substantial manor house with heavy stone mullioned windows and massive ornamental chimneys. There were, in the hall and parlour, stained glass windows with the arms of the Russells, de la Tours and the families into which they had married. The glass was removed and taken to Woburn in 1751. In 1794, or possibly a little before, Berwick was let to the Bryants who were there until well into this century, latterly as owners.

SWYRE – Holy Trinity Church

John Hutchins, the Dorset historian, was instituted as Rector of Swyre in 1729. Later he was Rector of Melcombe Horsey and of Holy Trinity, Wareham, but continued, nominally, to hold the Swyre living. He died in 1773.

His list of Rectors at Swyre begins with John de Candel, in 1297, but there had been parsons before him – the records of the Diocese do not give details of them before the very end of the 13th century. Elsewhere, a 'Richard, parson of Suere' is recorded in 1287. Generally, the patrons were disinterested, absentee landlords of a church poorly served by absentee parsons. It is not surprising that by the early 1800s 'neglect and maladministration, ecclesiastical as well as civil, attracted the notice of the Bishop and a resident curate was insisted on as well as a new parsonage house'.

Hutchins had been obliged to repair the chancel of the 14th century church at his own expense and, not long after, it was completely rebuilt by one of his successors. The nave was rebuilt in 1843 by the then Duke of Bedford. At the same time, some repairs were carried out on the tower, uncovering an arch corresponding to that of the chancel which had been plastered over. Only the two arches and the tower remain part of the mediæval building.

On either side of the south door is a stone with a carved shield-of-arms, each with a brass plate beneath. They were originally in the Berwick pew and moved when the church was restored. One commemorates James Russell and Alys (Wise), his wife, with the arms of Russell and Wise, the other, John Russell and Elizabeth (Frocksmer) with the arms of the two families. James was the father of the 1st Duke of Bedford and may have been John Russell's son, though this is not certain. The record seems sound but, in fact, the brass gives James as dying in 1509 when his will was proved in 1505. Both brasses have been shown to be in a script with Elizabethan rather than Tudor characteristics and it has been suggested that they were put up by the second Duke, who felt that the burial place of his forbears should be recorded, the lapse of time accounting for the error in the date.

In the chancel, on the north wall, is a monument in memory of the founder of the Napiers in England and of the family generally. It was erected by Sir Robert Napier, whose own memorial is on the south wall of Puncknowle Church. That, in Swyre, records that 'James Napier, who lyes here interred, came into England in the reign of Henry VIIth, settled here and supplied the several adjacent abbies with fish, from whom are descended the Napiers of Dorset and Somerset'. Sir Robert Napier, almost 200 years later, must have been sure of the fishmongers who were his ancestors but it does seem a strange way to set a family on the road to a baronetcy.

The wordy Latin of the brass plate at the west end of the church, is in memory of George and Mary Gollop of Berwick who had five sons and five daughters 'who lived to be men and women'. All were buried at Swyre in a family vault.

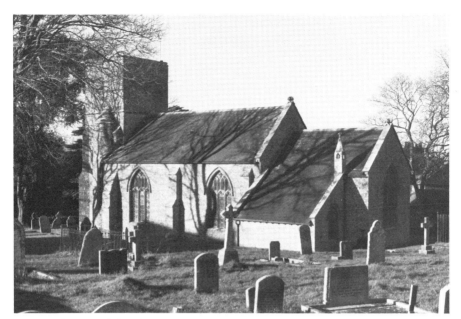

87. *Only the tower and chancel arch remain of the Swyre church built around 1400.*

88. *The James Russell brass in Swyre Church. 'Here lyeth James Russell, esquier, and Alys hys wyfe, daughter of John Wise, esquier, who decessyd the first yere of King Henry VIII. Anno MCCCCCIX'.*
Above: the rampant lion and three shells of the Russell family impale the three chevrons and crescent of that of Wise.

89. *Shipton Hill stands sentinel over the old village. Most of the houses have been modernised.*

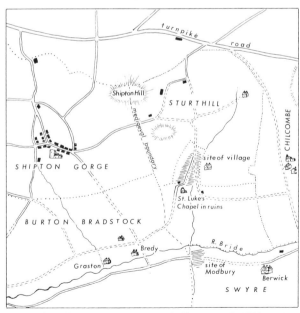

90. *Shipton Gorge and Sturthill village site in the 1700s.*

SHIPTON GORGE – Prehistoric and Roman

There are few evidences of prehistoric activity west of the chalk ridge, the heavy clays associated with the limestones being less attractive for settlement. One of the exceptions is Shipton Hill, an isolated greensand cap, which rises sharply, its shape like that of an upturned boat, some 60 ft. above the 500 ft. contour. The hill has been steepened on the north and south sides but the two ends form natural causeways leading up to the summit. The only rampart and ditch runs along the long sides but is not continued round the ends and is, unusually, at the foot of the hill. There is no doubt about the earthwork being of Iron Age date but it is best regarded as a lightly defended enclosure rather than a hill-fort (Fig. 3, 14). In the 1950s, W. Butcher, who was then at the nearby Higher Sturthill Farm, made a number of finds about the hill and carried out a small trial excavation. The pottery evidence suggests that occupation was mainly in the first phase of the Iron Age but the finding of a hoard of over 1000 slingstones must indicate a continuation into the 1st century BC and there is a possibility that there was activity in the area, if not on the hill, during the 1st century AD.

West of the village, against the boundary with Bothenhampton, is a Romano-British site (Fig. 3, No. 3) which was first suspected last century. It has never been excavated but its existence has been confirmed by further surface finds in recent years. The field in which it is situated is called Chisels (from an Old English word meaning gravel or pebbles) and probably refers to the slingstones, obviously collected from the Chesil Beach, which are turned up by the plough; they suggest that a Durotrigian settlement preceded that of the Romano-British period and this is confirmed by the coin evidence. As with other sites in the Bride Valley, the zenith of the Romano-British occupation was in the 3rd and 4th centuries and, like them, it is now virtually ploughed out. Enough has been found to justify the 'Romano-British building – site of' on the Ordnance Survey map. Over the years, more coins, pottery, glass, rings, brooches and domestic rubbish have been found, all related to the same period. Chisels is on a limestone promontory on the 400 ft. contour and the ground falls away sharply to the south and south-west, so that the site is unlikely to have been that of a villa.

Two stone heads found buried in a bank close to the village in 1958, are almost certainly Celtic cult-images. For the latter Iron Age Celts the head had a ritual importance which had grown out of their earlier practice of head-hunting. The so-called Celtic heads are recognised by their stylised representation of the features of the face. Those found at Shipton, together with the certain settlements on the hill-top and at Chisels suggest activity in the area which may have continued through the Dark Ages and emerged as the Anglo-Saxon Sepetona.

Hammilton Hill, to the south of Shipton Hill, is also a greensand cap but although crowned with a single Bronze Age barrow which points to activity in the vicinity in the second millenium BC, it does not appear to have been an occupation site.

SHIPTON GORGE – The Mediæval Manor

The mediæval village of Sepetona (sheep-farm) was almost in the centre of the Saxon manor, its boundary with Sterte, its neighbour on the east, running south from Shipton Hill; alone of the Bride Valley parishes, Shipton did not reach down to the river. In the Domesday Book, it was listed under a group of manors held by the King himself. Burton was also in the group which had to render 'one night's farm'; this was an ancient food-rent calculated to represent the supplies necessary to feed the King and his travelling Court for one day's stay. Since there was no individual entry for Shipton we cannot compare that manor with the others in the valley in the 11th century.

By the time of King John, Shipton was held by Thomas Maureward and, two centuries later, was still referred to as Shipton Maureward. That family lived at what is now Winterbourne Zelston and, of course, gave their name to Kingston Maurward near Dorchester. By 1285 we find the first use of Gorge in connection with Shipton. We have already met the two brothers, both named Ralph, and sons of Sir Thomas de Gorges who was Warden of Powerstock Castle. The younger became Lord of the Manor of Litton while the elder later, by marriage, came into extensive estates in Devon and Somerset, as well as the tiny manor of Shipton. While it is likely that the one lived in Litton, it is doubtful if the other was much concerned with Shipton, neither have we any record of the tenants who must have farmed there.

By the middle of the 15th century, the manor had passed, again by marriage, from the Gorges to the Copplestones, a Devon family. One, a Nicholas Copplestone, was almost certainly living at Shipton during the reign of Henry VIII. His great grandmother had been a Gorges who had married Lord Bonvil, and it was through him that the Copplestones held Shipton. At some time in the 17th century, it was bought by the Ilchester Estate and so continued until sold by them in 1910. This was at a time when many large estates were broken up into farms and a number of smallholdings; at Shipton, only the Manor Farm of some 200 acres remained of any size.

As we have seen, the holders of Shipton were generally absentee landlords but the Manor Court (where local disputes, especially those relating to the custom of the manor, were settled and, if necessary, judgement given) continued under the Copplestones and Ilchesters. By the 19th century, it was, however, as elsewhere, an outmoded formality.

E. J. Chaplin has found references to four common fields in the north, west, middle and south of the manor. He suggests that, because on the Tithe Map there were, at the beginning of the last century groups of fields incorporating the same name, enclosure at Shipton was gradual; it seems that the first step was to break the open land up into fields of something over 12 acres and to divide these later into smaller plots.

The various tenants of the manor would have lived in the Court House just to the west of the church. The field still bears the name Court and in it, according to Hutchins, were 'signs of fishponds and ruins'.

91.   *The church of St. Martin stands in an unusual position high above the old village.*

92.   *The view from the church across the old village to the housing estates of recent years. Of all the villages in the valley Shipton has shown most expansion.*

93. St. Martin's Church as rebuilt last century. Only the tower remains of the old building which Hutchins described as 'a small fabric containing nothing remarkable'.

94. The rather plain font with its seven-sided bowl must have survived from an earlier building. It pre-dates the 14th century tower by some 100 years.

SHIPTON – The Church of St. Martin

Anciently Shipton was part of the ecclesiastical parish of Burton but records linking the two are lacking. In the 13th century, Roger Kingeton was 'Rector of Brideton with the chapel of Bride (Bredy) annexed to the mother church'. It seems strange that, if there was a chapel at Shipton, it is not mentioned. However, the 13th century font survives, presumably from an earlier building and the tower is almost as old. The list of parsons serving Shipton is wanting because, at it was reported to a Church Commission in 1650, 'the Rectors of Burton have, time out of mind, found a minister to supply here at their own expense'. There was, however, no licence for burial at Shipton, although its population, by the time of Elizabeth, was almost as large as that of Burton. This must have caused considerable hardship and it seems that for a while in the early 1600s, they took matters into their own hands and paid their own parson and opened up the church for burial. In 1650 they were being persuaded to use Burton Church but objected because 'the inhabitants are not able to go to Burton church, the ways being impassable in winter and that Shipton is fit to be divided from Burton and be entire of itself, there being 250 persons in it and not one house within a mile of Burton'. But it was not to be – nearly 200 years passed before the churchyard of St. Martin's was in use again and not until recently did Shipton shake off the ecclesiastical shackles of Burton. The name St. Catherine's Cross persists for a spot on the road to Burton where, according to local tradition, the coffins were rested on their long journey to the graveyard.

The Royal Commission gives around 1400 for the date of the tower of St. Martin's. Hutchins described the church in 1735 as a small fabric, situated on an high ground, and consisting of a chancel, body and small north aisle, all tiled. Two galleries had been added, making 123 sittings possible. All this was swept away in 1861 by John Hicks, the Dorchester architect, who had a hand in the restoration of 27 Dorset churches, including nine completely new buildings; here he built a new church onto the old tower at a cost of just over £1000. The contractor was a local man who used stone from the quarries in the parish with dressings of that from Ham Hill and Bath. The carvings for the capitals and pulpit were among the earliest of many done for churches in the county by Benjamin Grassby of Dorchester. The new church was consecrated on August 6th, 1862.

From its high position on the south side, the church overlooked the old village with its cottages strung along the street in the little valley. A number of these, built in the 18th century, still exist, much modernised. They are in contrast to the recent bungalows and houses which, in turn, dominate them from the higher ridge to the west. The Court House has long since gone and the oldest building in the parish, apart from the church tower, is the 17th century Innsacre farmhouse on the road running north from the village. The Royal Commission also noted that Lower Sturthill Farmhouse, about one and half miles east of Shipton Church, has a 17th century east wing which retains some original stone-mullioned windows.

STURTHILL – The Lost Village

Between Shipton and Chilcombe on the east, lay the mediæval manor of Sterthill with its village on the tiny stream that rises at the foot of Chilcombe Hill and flows down to the Bride. It was the 'Sterte' of the Domesday Book with five hides and four ploughlands, one of the many Dorset manors then held by the wife of the Norman Earl Hugh Fitz-Grip who had dealt heavily with Saxon unrest in the county.

Sturthill was most probably later divided into two smaller manors; one, with its house at Uppesturtel near the source of the stream, so-called to distinguish it from Nether or Lower Sturtel further down the valley. References to the village in the 14th century, almost always use the latter name. The Diocesan list of the rectors and their patrons from 1298 to 1545, gives a clue to the mediæval holders of the manor but very little is known of their tenants.

The terse statement in Hutchins 'in after ages it was divided into different parts' is vague but to the point. By the 16th century, the village had become so poor that it could no longer support its church and was 'united' with Burton. The division into smaller farms seems to have taken place at this time and it is likely that Upsturthill alone maintained its mediæval identity. Ecclesiastically, the parish was in Burton but later, for civil administrative purposes, it was divided between Shipton and Burton, increasing the size of the former parish almost twofold. The old village and the land to the south, went to Burton and the irregular parish boundaries of today probably result from an attempt to fit blocks of land under the same ownership into the same parish.

The site of St. Luke's Chapel is given on Ordnance Survey Maps. Hutchins, in 1735, saw remains of the building and traces of the churchyard wall. These have long since vanished and today nothing is left to indicate the site. In the 1970s, fieldwork by the writer confirmed the position of the wall and graveyard with the hollow-way (now a bridle path) of the village street running round the north side, in the little field known as Chapel Close. At that time, it was impossible to find any trace of the village, but subsequent deep ploughing of the adjacent field showed the main street with its cottages to have been north of the chapel; a lane continued up over the hill, past what is now St. Luke's Farm, to the main road. The modern bridleways which, for no apparent reason, converge in the middle of a field, can now be shown to follow the old roads which showed clearly in the plough-soil.

The chapel must have been small, it is likely that all three original mediæval churches, Shipton, Sturthill and Chilcombe were comparable in size. Hutchins described it as a small building consisting of a body in which are three windows, two doors on the north and south sides and one (unusually) on the east. After the closing of the church in 1545, the tithes continued to be paid to a lay impropriator. Some of the Lower Sturthill land, with the old village, was added to the Bedford's Berwick Farm over the Bride for which the estate paid £6 a year to the former St. Luke's Rectory.

95. The site of the mediæval village of Sturthill lies just below the centre of the photograph. In the distance Lower Sturthill Farm marks the position of mediæval Uppesturtel.

96. The field in the centre is still Chapel Close. The church was just to the left of the shed. Beneath the field in the foreground are traces of a Romano-British settlement.

97. *This track, now impassable except on foot, was the accepted way from Burton village to the beach and was regularly used by carts bringing up fish and gravel. Bind Barrow is the hill on the left.*

98. *Frequent flooding back up to the village has built up the valley floor with silt. The settlement grew up on the higher ground to the north.*

BURTON BRADSTOCK – Early Settlement

Three round barrows were noted in the parish by the Royal Commission but, without excavation, there is some doubt about their identification. Bind Barrow, overlooking the beach, is the most familiar but the second element of the name could equally refer to the hill itself. A mile or so to the east of Bind Barrow, Greenhill is a limestone spur jutting out from the coastal ridge, northwards to the valley. This was the site of another of the Durotrigian/ Romano-British settlements in the area (Fig. 3, No. 13). It was first noted towards the end of the last century when burials were dug out of the workings of a quarry, together with their accompanying food-vessels. Further finds, including Samian ware, have since been found but the site is now ploughed out. In the village itself, near the Anchor Inn, building trenches in 1963 exposed similar burials and pottery while, at Freshwater, yet more evidence has been found in soil eroded from the low cliffs (Fig. 3, Nos. 1/2).

Brideport and Brideton

There are seven Burton place names in Dorset and more still elsewhere in the country. The word, as a rule, signifies a farm (ton) near an earthwork (burh) but our Burton is an exception, the first element of the name coming from the River Bride. Thus it is the Anglo-Saxon 'farm on the Bride'; Bradstock comes from Bradenstoke, a mediæval priory in North Wiltshire, which once held the church and, probably, some lands in the parish.

A fascinating problem is presented by the relationship of the town of Bridport to the River Bride. Settlements along a river often take their names from it; along the Bride we have Brideton (Burton), Bredy, Longbredy and Little Bredy. Bridport seems, at first glance, to be named after the River Brit or Brid on which it stands; there are, however, no 'Brid' place names up the valley of that little river. Instead, the names are all derived from the old name of the river which was Wooth (e.g. Aqua de Woth, the Wooth Water of 1287). They include Watton, Wooth Manor, Binghams Farm (which was Binghams Worth) and Camesworth. Place name experts agree that the name of the River Brit came from the town name and not, as usually happened, the other way round.

It seems certain, therefore, that the 'Brid' element in Bridport is, as shown by its early form 'Brideport', really that of the River Bride. We should remember, as well, that the extension of Bridport Borough down to the sea, is relatively recent and that Burton Bradstock's western boundary was with Symondsbury along the Brit, at what is now West Bay. We have already discussed the problem of fixing the site of King Alfred's stronghold 'in Brydian' (page 10). Recent work by The Rev. Basil Short, has identified the original Saxon Brideport as a small town, probably 'walled' with an earthen rampart, built across the river, its harbour one and quarter miles up-stream from the later one at the river mouth. The most likely explanation seems to be that Old Warren, at Little Bredy, was the original hill-top 'burh', its defences, perhaps, never completed before it was moved to a defended harbour-site in the Wooth Valley. Keeping its name, Brydian or Bride, it soon became Brideport to distinguish it from its older neighbour Brideton and, later, gave its name to its own river.

BURTON BRADSTOCK – The Manors

At the time of the Domesday Survey, Bridetona was divided into a large manor which was part of a group held by the King (as we have seen under Shipton), and a smaller, including the church, which was held by the abbey of St. Wandrille in Normandy. Early in the 12th century, the crown land was given by Henry I to the abbey of St. Stephen in Caen, also in Normandy, partly for the redemption of his soul and partly in return for the handing back of the crown and royal ornaments which his father had given that abbey. Burton thus became attached to the Benedictine Priory of Frampton, which was a cell of the Norman abbey. Like some other mediæval landowners in the valley, as we have already seen, the Prior had his troubles, as in 1287 he had to take Peter, parson of the church of St. Mary at Bridport, and Thomas de Lodres to court for 'taking growing corn at Brideton'. The priory held Burton until 1437 when, the foreign monasteries having been suppressed, it was given by Henry VI to the Royal College of St. Stephen, Westminster.

Hutchins says that St. Wandrille held only the advowson of the church but records show that land was included with it. In 1286, these were exchanged for lands held in Normandy by the Wiltshire Priory of Bradenstoke which explains the second element of the name of the village. In 1292, the lands held by its Prior were valued at £4 6s. 8d., which may be compared with the £12 13s. 4d. of the old crown manor lands then held by the Priory of Frampton. The last presentation to the church by Bradenstoke was in 1469, after which the patrons were the Dean and Canons of St. Stephens, Westminster, so that it seems that about this time, the two parts of Burton came together.

After the Dissolution it was held briefly by the Crown and, in 1579, Christopher Hatton is recorded as holding the advowson. By the end of Elizabeth's reign, together with the manor, it had passed to Sir Thomas Freke and then, via the Pitts, to Lord Rivers in the 1700s. These families were all related by marriage and eventually Burton, in the later 1800s, became part of the estate of Augustus Henry Lane-Fox-Pitt-Rivers which extended over 24,492 acres in Dorset and 2762 acres in Wiltshire. In fact, it was said that he could, before it was in part sold off, have ridden from his house at Rushmore in North Dorset to the sea at Burton without leaving his own land. He died in 1900, internationally regarded as the founder of modern archaeology and was succeeded by his eldest son, with whose death in 1928, much of the property was sold. Burton, however, survived until 30 years later, when it was put on the market and, what has been described as 'one of Burton's golden ages' came to an end.

The ecclesiastical parish of Burton has always included Graston and Bredy, both distinct mediæval manors. The end of the village of Sturthill led to a complicated division of its tithes as well as its land, some of which, as we have seen, was added to Burton. Until the late 1700s, Litton was the largest parish in the valley, both in population and in acreage but, by 1839, although the sizes remained the same, Burton's population had increased almost twofold to over 1000, mainly because of the introduction of spinning mills; today, the differential is maintained and the rateable value of Burton is far and away higher than that of any of the other villages.

99. *The view across the old village to the modern housing beyond Annings Lane. The road and hedge line running from bottom left to centre may well be the boundary between the two manors.*

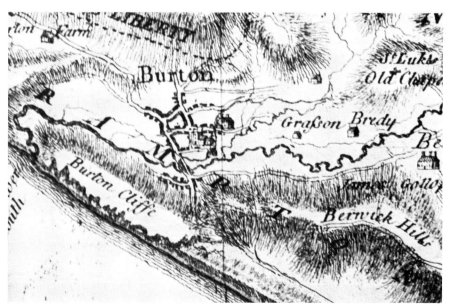

100. *Burton as shown on Isaac Taylor's map of Dorset in 1765.*

101. *Burton has a fair number of cottages which have survived from the 17th century, often altered or extended. The Three Horseshoes is a good example.*

102. *The Roberts' Grove Mill has been converted into housing. A plaque on the wall reads 'This flax-swingling mill the first introduced into the west of England was erected by Richards Roberts 1803'.*

BURTON BRADSTOCK – The Village

The Anglo-Saxon Brideton followed a Romano-British settlement on the higher ground just north of the river. Just how the manors of the two priories were divided is not known for certain, but an ancient boundary appears to run southwards from Bennett's Hill Farm down to Shadrach Farm and then straight on as the High Street and Cliff Road. The land between this and the mediæval Graston may have been the original Bradenstoke manor.

Like the other villages along the coast, the main occupation of Burton was with the land, combined with the seasonal fishing from the beach. From the 17th century, Burton had the reputation of providing men both for the Royal Navy and for the ships trading with the newly established colonies. This local association with sea-going may have been further influenced by the fact that West Dorset, with Bridport as centre, had, from the 13th century, grown and manufactured hemp and flax for cordage and sails. Burton has always been associated with the cottage netting industry and, indeed, an attempt was made in the early 1500s to set up a rope-walks, but this did not succeed because in 1530 an Act of Parliament prohibited anyone living within five miles of Bridport from making rope.

From 1794 to 1840, however, the quiet association of cottage industry farming and fishing was rudely interrupted by the Roberts family, who combined the former with the manufacture of flax. It was Richard Roberts who, having married a well-to-do Burton widow, set up a water-driven spinning mill in 1794, just south of the church. In 1803, further up the river, he built Grove Mill, near Grove House, which had been brought to him by his wife. This was a swingling mill replacing the age-old industry of separating the fibres by hand. His third mill, built near the first in 1813, was intended for finer spinning. Their products ranged from sail cloth to table napkins and from hammocks to tea towels. Some 50 men and women from the village were employed, but Roberts also used child labour, seeking boys and girls from workhouses, both far and near, preferring the younger girls as being generally the best workers and more obedient to command. These pauper apprentices were housed and fed in sheds which have since disappeared; they worked 'not more than twelve hours a day' and were sent to the parson for two hours every Sunday to be 'taught to read and say their catechism'. All this seems very harsh, but Roberts appears to have been a just employer at a time when child labour was an accepted practice.

By 1840, the unrestricted import of raw materials, together with a lack of real interest by his sons, brought the Roberts' business to an end. By 1843, the Grove Mill was converted to grinding corn and continued to do so for another 100 years, the spinning mills carrying on with a succession of owners and varying output, the final closure coming in 1931. Meanwhile, at Burton, as elsewhere in the Bride Valley, the womenfolk supplemented the family income with their cottage netmaking as outworkers for the Bridport factories.

In 1958, the sale of the Pitt-Rivers Estate marked the beginning of a change and a period of growth. The village's charm, for the ever-increasing number of holidaymakers, lies in the number of 16th and 17th century thatched cottages which still remain, albeit much modernised, as its nucleus. They contrast with the modern housing estates, but, like them, are now mostly occupied by older, retired people from far afield.

BURTON BRADSTOCK – The Church of St. Mary

Very few Dorset churches are mentioned in the Domesday Survey but Burton was one of them and was recorded, with Bridport, as held by the Norman abbey of St. Wandrille. It may not be mere coincidence that both have the same Norman cruciform plan and both are dedicated to St. Mary.

At Burton the oldest part of the existing church is the north wall of the nave with two original 14th century windows. The corresponding south wall was demolished in 1897 when it was replaced, by E. S. Prior, with an arcade and the south aisle added. The tower and two transepts were built in the 15th century and the chancel some hundred years after that. The roofs of the nave and transepts have barrel-vaults with carved bosses.

Hutchins' list of Rectors begins with Robert de la Wyle being presented in 1295. He also suggests that the grant of the church to St. Wandrille was in respect of the advowson only but 13th century records show that land was also involved. Thus in 1302 a jury had to decide whether 67 acres of land (i.e. ploughland), seven acres of meadow and a dwelling-house belonged to the parson as a free gift pertaining to the church of Brideton or whether it was part of the lay fee of the Priory of Bradenstoke.

Shipton, as we have seen, was served from Burton and was recorded as a chapel-of-ease in the Return of the Church Commission in 1650. No mention, however, is made of a St. Laurence's Chapel said to have been just to the north of the church and where, according to tradition many human bones were dug up. It does seem unlikely that Burton needed two churchyards almost side by side since, in mediæval times, burial ground was used over and over again. Hutchins, moreover, himself wrote around 1730 'the church of Burton is dedicated to the Blessed Virgin Mary or, as the inhabitants say, to St. Laurence'. There are only two records relating to the chapel of St. Laurence, both of them in the time of Elizabeth and within a few years of each other. It is just possible that they refer in fact to the parish church under an earlier dedication.

There was certainly, a mediæval chapel-of-ease at Bredy which must then have had a sufficient population to warrant its own little church. In the early 1300s Roger Kyngeton was 'Rector of Brideton with the chapel of Bride annexed to the mother church'. Soon after there was a protracted legal argument between the Prior of Bradenstoke and Thomas de Bonevill as to who should present the parson to the church of Bryde Bonevill – from the latter name it will be seen that Thomas was Lord of the Manor of Bredy at that time. The jury found in favour of the Prior and so the attempt to make Bredy Chapel a rectory in its own right failed and it remained united to St. Mary's at Burton. There is, however, no further mention of it and it is likely that, with the decline of the population following the plague, by the end of the century it was no longer needed.

Yet another chapel is mentioned, albeit briefly, in Burton parish in the 17th century – St. Catherine's which traditionally gave its name to St. Catherine's Cross on the Shipton road. Whether the latter marks the site of a chapel, a wayside cross, or is just the name of the former crossroads is a matter for conjecture.

103. The massive crossing tower of the church of St. Mary the Virgin overshadows the rest of the building.

104. Church, rectory and former non-conformist chapel form an attractive group.

105. Hutchins' description of Graston still holds good – anciently a manor and hamlet, now a single farmhouse.

106. Bredy. The Paulet's house was replaced by the present building when the Hussey family owned the manor early last century. The site of the mediæval chapel is unknown but it must be near the house.

BURTON BRADSTOCK – Graston and Bredy

Graston Farm, on the little stream running down to the Bride from Shipton, marks the site of the hamlet of the mediæval manor. It is the Gravstan of the Domesday Book, the second element of the name meaning stone; the first, though uncertain may indicate the grey colour of the stone, perhaps used as a boundary mark. In 1086 it was held 'of the wife of Hugh' by the same tenant as held Sturthill, paid geld for two and a half hides and had land for two ploughs. With its mill and 16 acres of meadow it was valued at 60 shillings.

By the 13th century part of it at least was held by Abbotsbury Abbey; at an inquest in 1268 as to the rights and privileges of the Abbot, a gift to the monastery of one ploughland in Graveston was recorded. With additional land in nearby Shipton it continued to be held by the Abbey until the Dissolution, when, in 1545 it was granted by Henry VIII to none other than John Russell, the Berwick farmer's son who was now Lord Russell, Comptroller of the King's Household and second only in seniority to the Treasurer. From then on Graston followed the usual pattern of a succession of tenants and later of owners. In the 18th century it was bought by the Strodes of Parnham and 100 years later belonged, together with its neighbour Bredy, to the Hussey family.

For some reason Hutchins overlooked the Domesday Book entry for Bridie which was held by Berenger Giffard 'of the King'. Somewhat larger than Graston it was taxed for four hides and there was land for three ploughs. Around 1300 the manor was held by the Bonvil family who gave Bredy its old name Bonvil's Bredy. We have already noted the argument between them and the Prior of Bradenstoke over the chapel at Bridie. In 1320 it was recorded that, 'the Sheriff has several times to cause to come here twelve of the view of Brydyebonevill, who are not related to the Prior of Bradenstoke, to recognise that right the said Prior has in the advowson of the church'. The Prior eventually proved his point and the attempt by Thomas Bonvil to make his Bredy Chapel a separate church was shortlived. In Tudor times the farm was held by the Mores of Melplash and their successors, the Paulets, most likely lived at Bredy in the 17th century. Hutchins wrote that the Paulets built the house 'as appeared by their arms on the side of it'. One hundred years later it was described as 'long since reduced to a farmhouse and much of it pulled down'.

We have noted under Chilcombe how Francis and Mary Roberts settled there in the early 1700s. In 1734 their son, Francis, took over Hembury Farm over the hill in the Asker Valley and later moved back to Bredy, having married well into a Loders farming family. One of the sons of that marriage was the Richard Roberts who was responsible for Burton's short venture into the spinning and weaving industry; his brother Robert, having farmed elsewhere in the Bride Valley, eventually leased Cogden Farm on the Ridge between Bredy and the sea.

Traces of the mediæval hamlet of Bredy can still be seen and the old road, with its ford over the river, is marked by a hollow-way on the east side of the Bride. The site of the mediæval chapel is not known. Like others elsewhere it was probably used as a farm building before becoming altogether lost.

The reader will have been aware of a gap in the story of the valley. Here, as elsewhere in England, the archaeological sequence seems to end abruptly with the end of the Roman Occupation, so that how and where people were living during the so-called Dark Ages is one of archaeology's intriguing problems. It would seem, however, that the discovery of so many Iron Age and Romano-British sites close to or within the Anglo-Saxon villages must point to some form of continuity.

By the Domesday Survey of 1086 the village pattern was already firmly established and we have a picture of small communities whose life was intimately bound up with, as well as dominated by, the agricultural economy of the mediæval manor. It is likely that the landscape as we know it was already emerging by the end of the 12th century. The lynchets and abandoned fields on slopes where cultivation seems impossible are evidence of the need to feed the expanding population of the next 150 years. This was followed by the decline brought about in the main by the Black Death which we know struck heavily in the valley. In the following years sheep farming increased at the expense of arable land and the valley must have carried many of the 6000 strong flock owned by Cerne Abbey in 1535.

The years following the dissolution of the monasteries saw the rise of new land-owning families, some of them former tenant farmers who now had the opportunity to buy land they had once rented. Such were the Hurdings of Longbredy and the Hodders of Litton. Other older-established families moved into the valley to acquire land and this continued into the 18th century with the Napiers at Puncknowle, the Michels at Longbredy and the Mellors at Littlebredy. The slightly later Williams estate which followed the Mellors is the only one to survive intact.

The last century saw village life reach its peak. Each community was inward-looking towards its own craftsmen – brewer, baker, blacksmith, shoemaker, butcher, wheelwright, carpenter, schoolmaster – all these were represented at Litton in 1859. The beginning of the present century brought little change until the impact of the First World War and the subsequent rapid development of the motor car had their effect.

The decades following the Second World War, well within living memory, have been marked by the acceleration of change common to the whole of the country and this still continues. Mechanisation of farming has taken the place of the workforce once necessary and the few younger people living in the villages find work mainly in the towns. With the modernisation of old cottages and the building of new houses, particularly where mains drainage has been provided, the drift of working people away from the villages has been compensated by an influx of retired couples seeking refuge from city life. Happily a new kind of village is emerging combining the old and the new; sadly it lacks that sense of interdependence which was once the hallmark of village life.

107. *The Bride as it enters Burton Bradstock.*

108. *Freshwater. The Bride has no visible mouth, the water percolating through the shingle bank from a small lagoon. The coincidence of a high tide, south-west wind and heavy rainfall always leads to flooding back up the stream towards Burton.*

109. The Bride Valley as shown on the 1886 reprint of the first 1 in. to the mile Ordnance Survey map of 1811.

APPENDIX A

Archaeological Sites

Page 4. Fig. 3. Map references.

Iron Age/Romano-British sites with no surface features remaining

1. Burton Freshwater	SY 479895	8. Longbredy	SY 568902
2. Burton Village	SY 486895	9. Littlebredy	SY 582888
3. Chisels, Shipton	SY 484919	10. Walls, Puncknoll	SY 540873
4. Sturthill	SY 514908	11. Puncknowle Knoll	SY 534882
5. Higher Coombe	SY 536916	12. Oxclose, Swyre	SY 516892
6. Pins Knoll, Litton	SY 541905	13. Greenhill, Burton	SY 512886
7. Litton Village	SY 554908		

For further reference see the writer's paper 'Settlement Patterns in the Bride Valley' in Vol. 102 of the Society's *Proceedings,* 1980.

Sites scheduled under the Ancient Monuments Act

Hill-forts

14. Shipton Hill	SY 588922	16. Old Warren	SY 585886
15. Chilcombe Hill	SY 530920	17. Abbotsbury Castle	SY 556866

Other sites

A. Litton Cheney earth circle	SY 556917
B. Martin's Down barrow group	SY 570910
C. Blackdown barrow group	SY 572912
D. Poor Lot barrow group	SY 590900
E. Valley of Stones Celtic fields	SY 597874
F. Tenants Hill enclosure and stone circle	SY 578880
G. Mare and Colts long barrow	SY 585870

References to the scheduled monuments are included in general works on the archaeology of the county in particular:

Royal Commission on Historical Monuments, *Dorset,* Vol. 1, 1952.

L. V. Grinsell, *Archaeology of Wessex,* Methuen, 1958.

L. V. Grinsell, *Dorset Barrows,* DNH&AS, 1959.

All have from time to time been considered in the *Proceedings* of the Society as well as in the appropriate national archaeological journals.

A SUMMARY OF THE RETURNS OF THE DOMESDAY SURVEY FOR THE BRIDE VALLEY IN 1086

	Tax assessment in hides	Plough teamlands	Peasants	Value of mill	Value before 1066	Value 1086
Littlebredy	11	6	16	–	£16	£16
Longbredy	9	9	19	6s.	£22	£22
Litton	10	8	20	30d.	£6	£9
Puncknowle	5	4	13	12s.	£3	£5
Bexington	9½	7	20	–	£4	£6
Swyre	9	7	21	–	£9	£9
Chilcombe	3	3	14	5s.	£3	£3
Sturthill	5	4	10	6s.	£4	£5
Bredy	4	3	14	10s.	£3	£4
Graston	2½	2	11	7s.	£2	£3

Details for Burton and Shipton are not known as they are hidden in in the collective return for a group of royal manors which also included Bere Regis, Bradpole and Chideock. Kingston may also have been included in such a group. Litton is not named in the survey; the figures given are for a manor whose Saxon owner was given as two brothers and which was in the Hundred of Uggescombe.

The teamland figures enable us to compare the agricultural potential of the manors since they represent the number of plough teams of eight oxen necessary if all the land available was taken into cultivation. The figures for Littlebredy show that much land was unploughed (see page 11).

The mill was an important mediæval asset and a prerogative of the Lord of the Manor. All the mills mentioned in the survey could have been on the Bride itself – indeed the pattern of land distribution suggests that access to the main stream was an important factor when the boundaries were determined.

BIBLIOGRAPHY

General works on Dorset with some reference to the Bride Valley.

Brocklebank, J.   *Victorian Stone Carvers in Dorset Churches* (1979).
Fagersten, A.   *Place Names of Dorset* (1933).
Gardner, D.   *Companion into Dorset* (1939).
Good, R.   *The Old Roads of Dorset* (1966).
Good, R.   *The Lost Villages of Dorset* (1979).
Harvey Darton, F. J.   *Alibi Pilgrimage* (1936).
Hutchins, J.   *The History and Antiquities of Dorset,* 3rd Edn., Vol. 2 (1863).
Kerr, B.   *Bound to the Soil* (1968).
Newman, J. and Pevsner, N.   *The Buildings of England – Dorset* (1972).
Notes and Queries for Somerset and Dorset (1888 onwards).
Oswald, A.   *The Country Houses of Dorset* (1935).
The Victoria History of the County of Dorset, Vol. 2 (1908), Vol. 3 (1968).
Proceedings of the Dorset Natural History and Archaeological Society (yearly 1877-1980).
Royal Commission on
    Historical Monuments   Vol. 1, *West Dorset* (1952).

Books or pamphlets relating specifically to the Bride Valley.

Chaplin, E. J.   *Shipton Gorge* (1980).
Daniell, E. S.   *The Valley of the Bride* (1950).
Dittmer, A. R.   *A Short History of Burton Bradstock* (1963).
Eastwood, J.   *The Burton Bradstock Book* (1974).
Long, E. T.   *The Churches of Burton Bradstock, Chilcombe and Shipton Gorge* (1969).
Moon, A. A.   *Notes on the History and Architecture of West Bexington* (1969).
Trotman, E. F.   *The Rectors of Longbredy in Dorset* (1968).

Much use has been made of material in the County Record Office and in the library of the County Museum. The latter's large collection of unpublished transcriptions of Public Record Office documents of the Middle Ages and its manuscript volumes relating to the Tudor and Stuart periods have helped add to the picture of the Bride Valley's past. The card index deposited in the Museum Library details all references to them in this book.